Mastering Anime Art: Step-by-Step Guide to Drawing Anime Characters

This Book has Over 300 Detailed Illustrations That Demonstrate How to Draw Anime Step by Step

J.P. Manning

Copyright © 2024

Copyright © 2024

1. Drawing a basic grid outline will help you
to give your picture good proportions.

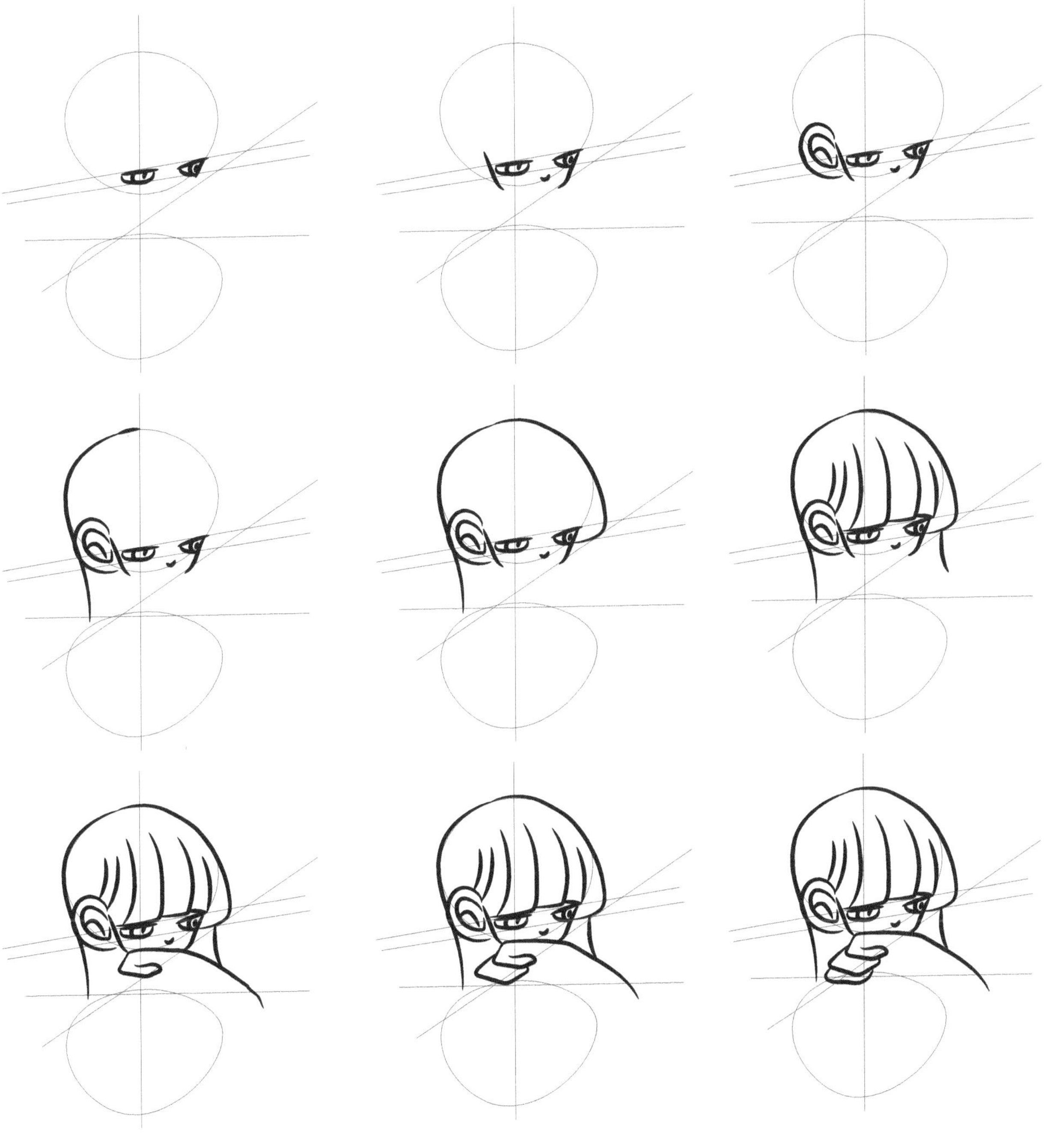

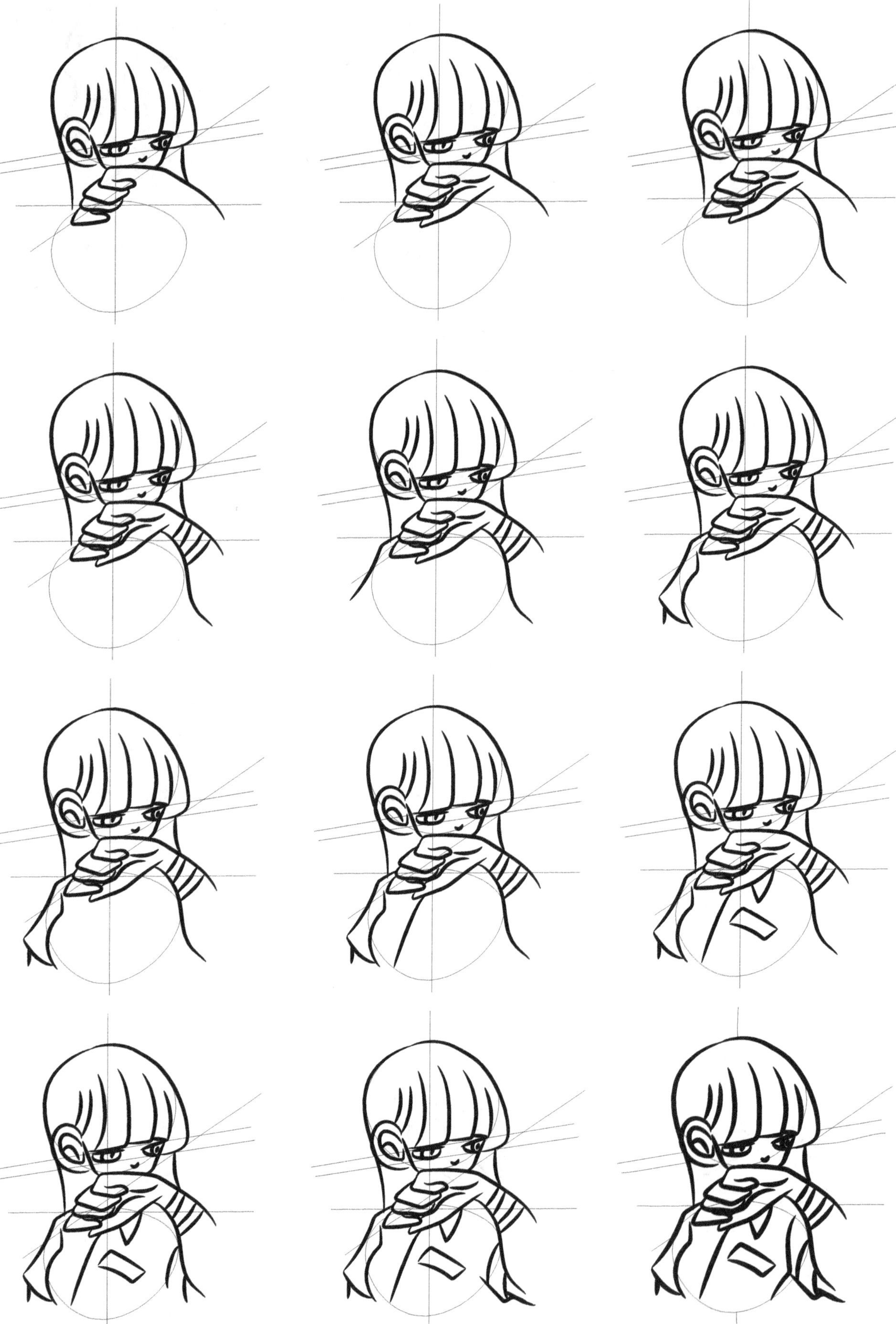

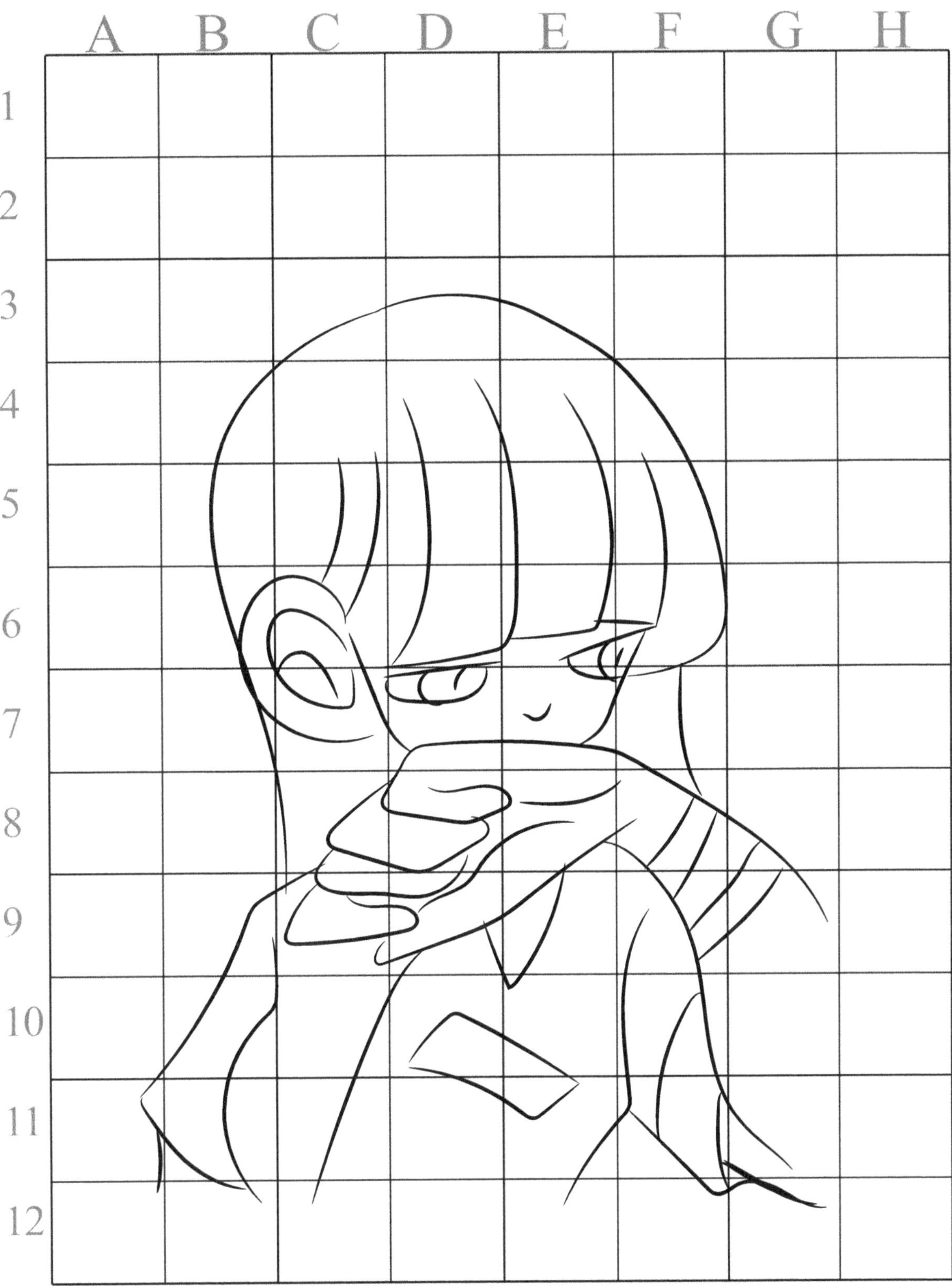

2. Starting your drawing with the eyes will help your initial sketch to take shape.

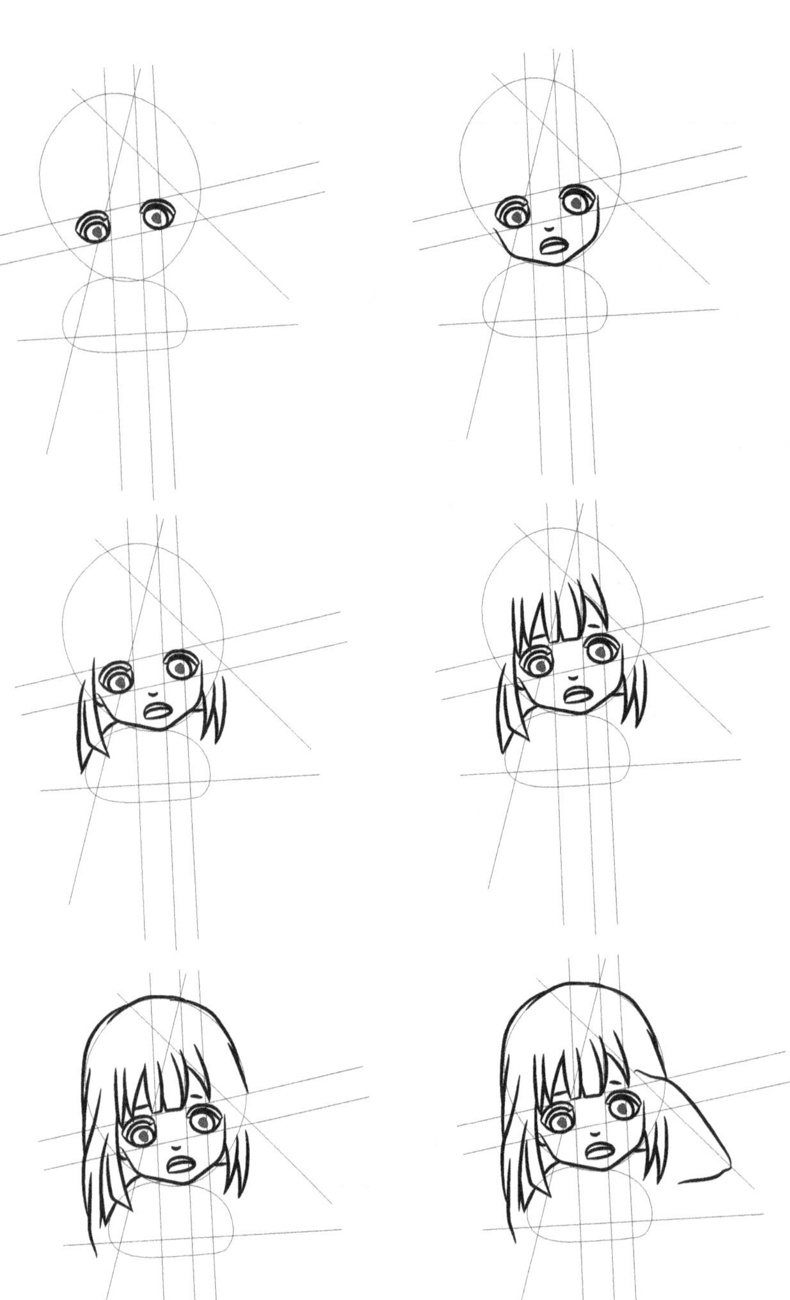

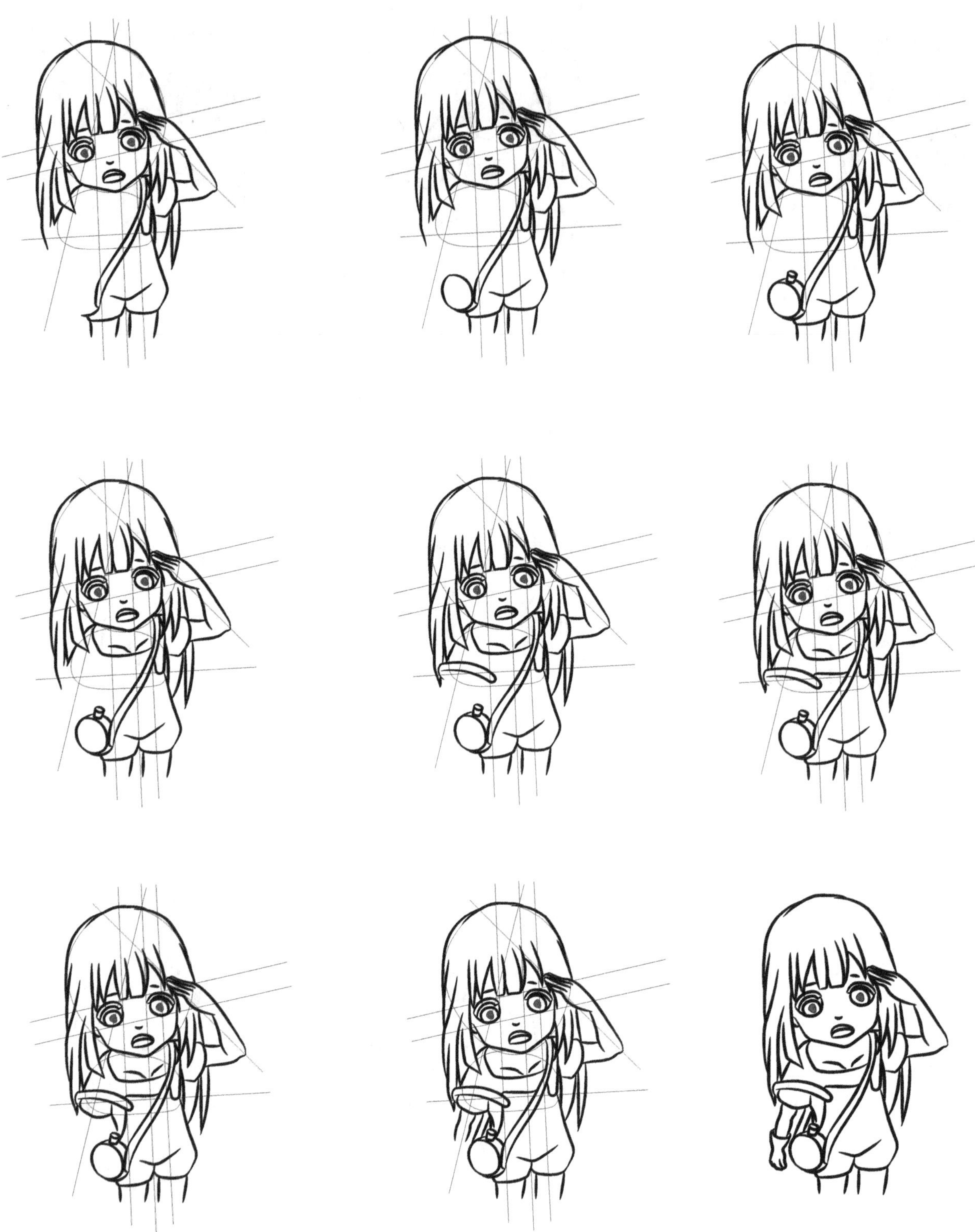

A B C D E F G H
1
2
3
4
5
6
7
8
9
10
11
12

3. Drawing eyes further apart can make your character look more passive.

 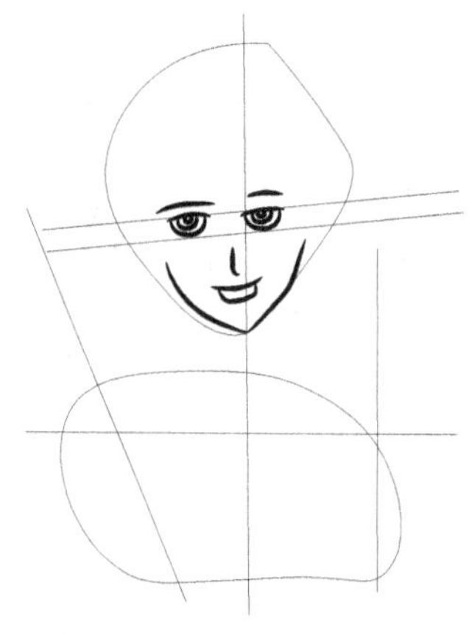 

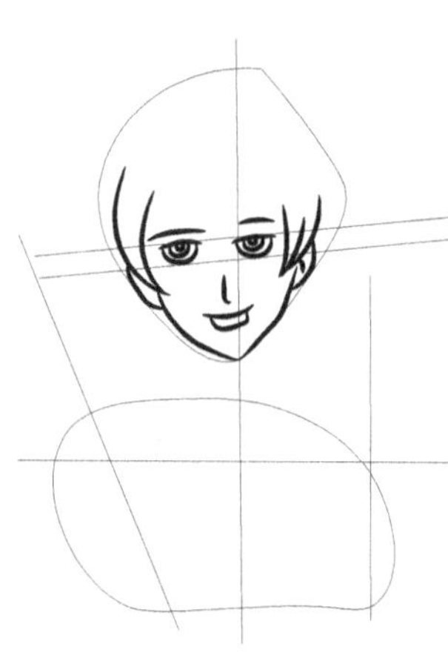  

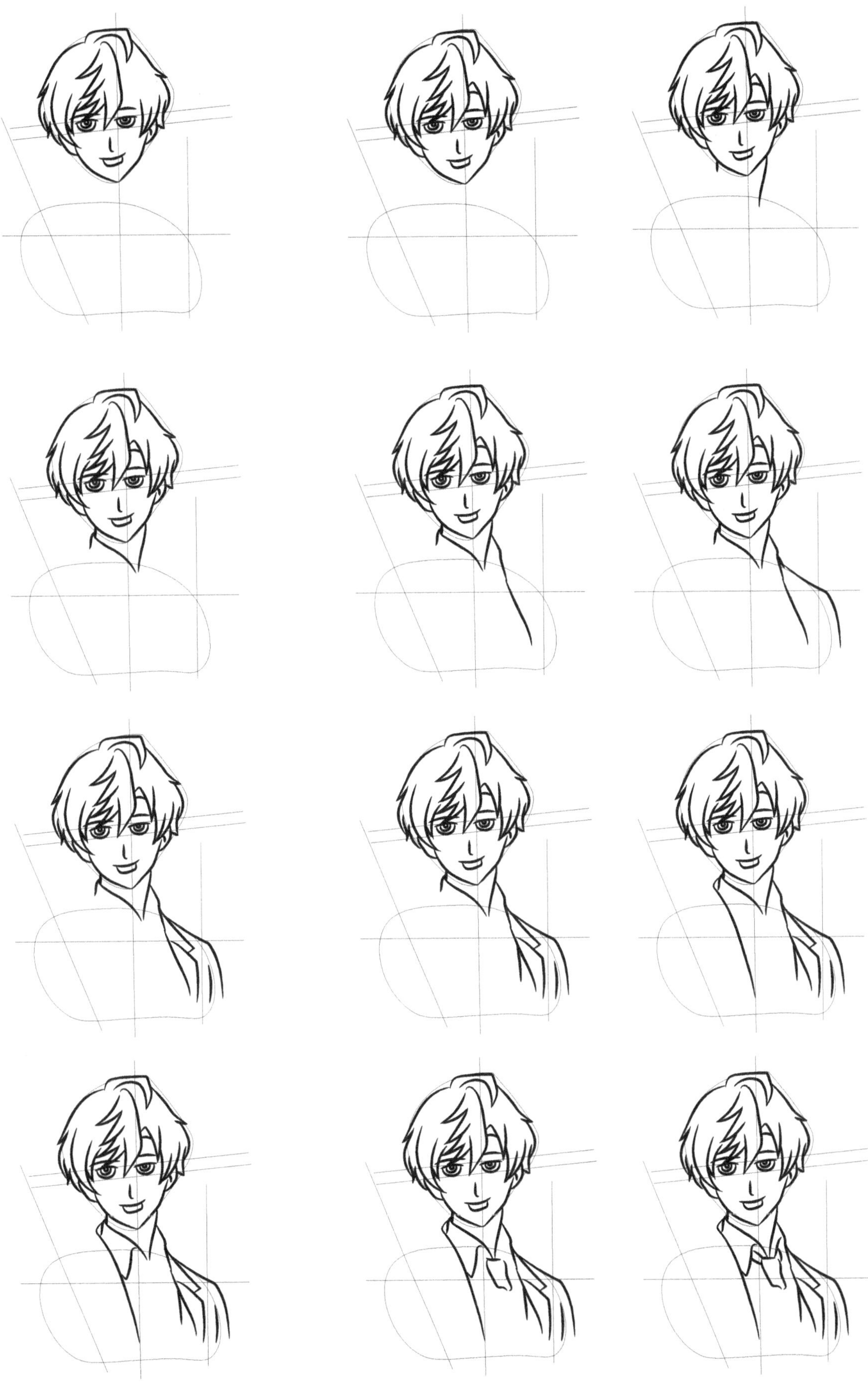

A B C D E F G H
1 2 3 4 5 6 7 8 9 10 11 12

4. Enlarging the eyes of your characters can make them look more childlike and vulnerable.

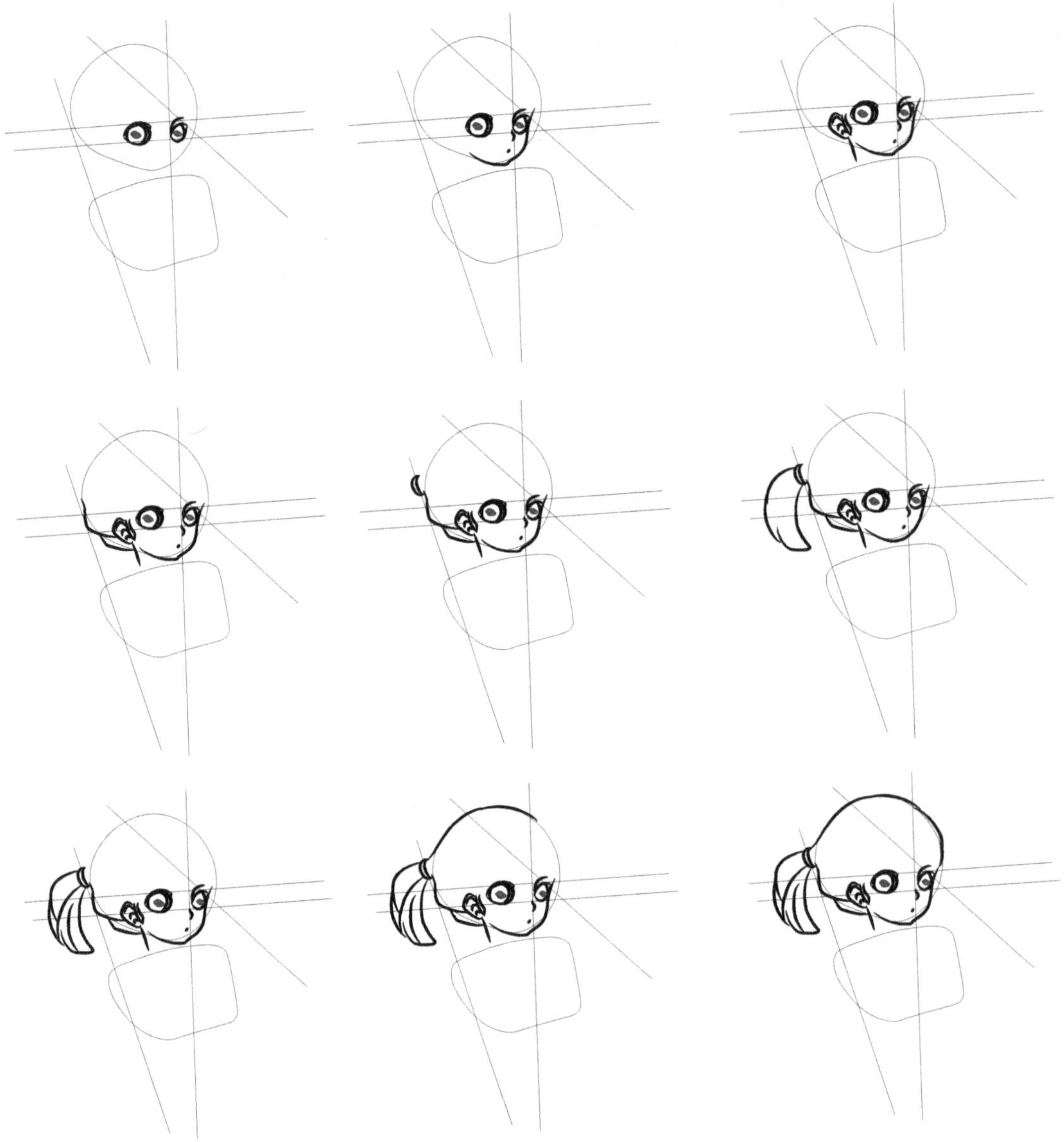

A B C D E F G H
1
2
3
4
5
6
7
8
9
10
11
12

5. Creating a grid with ellipses for the major joints and lines for the major bones can offer a structure to work around.

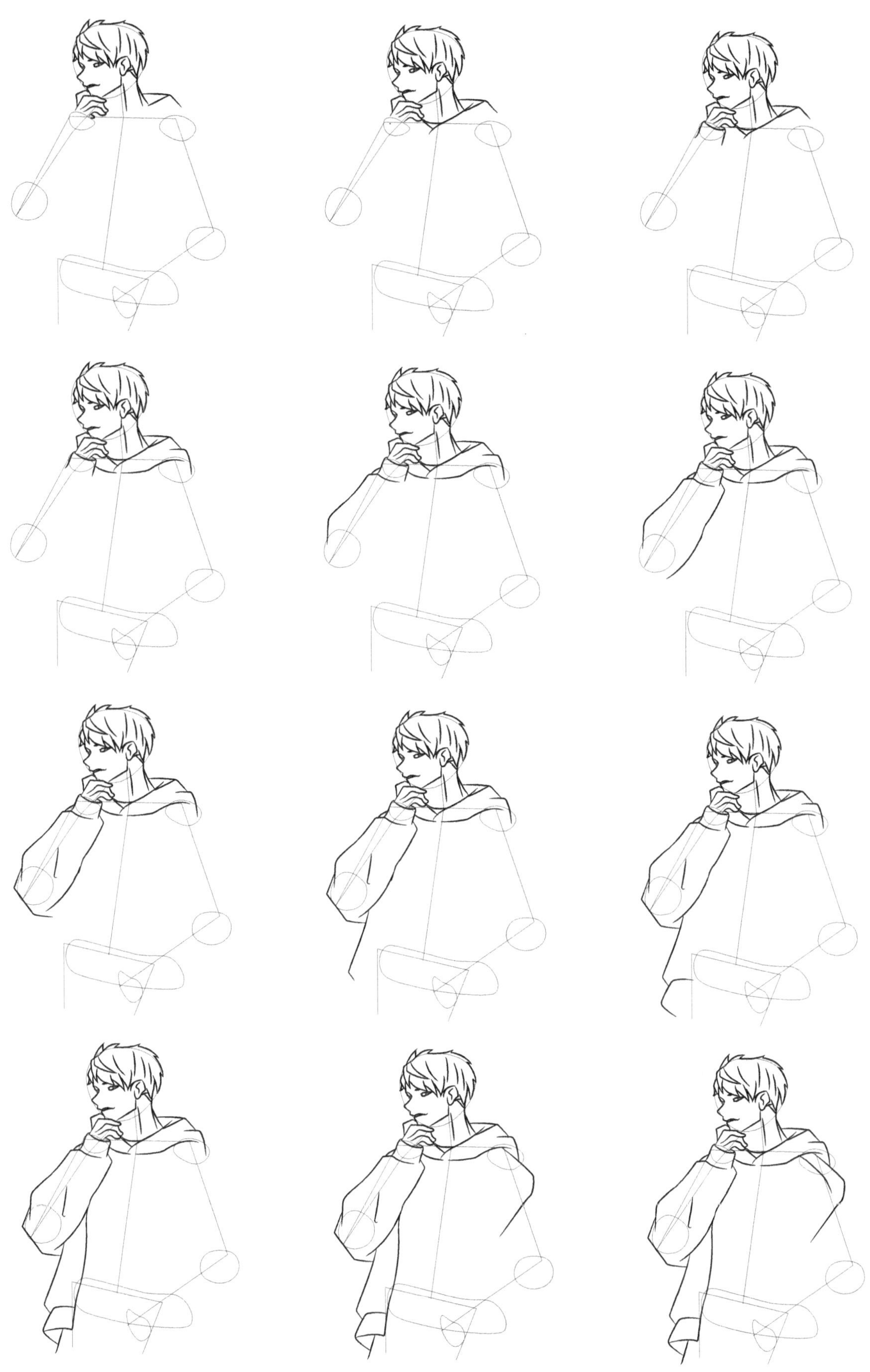

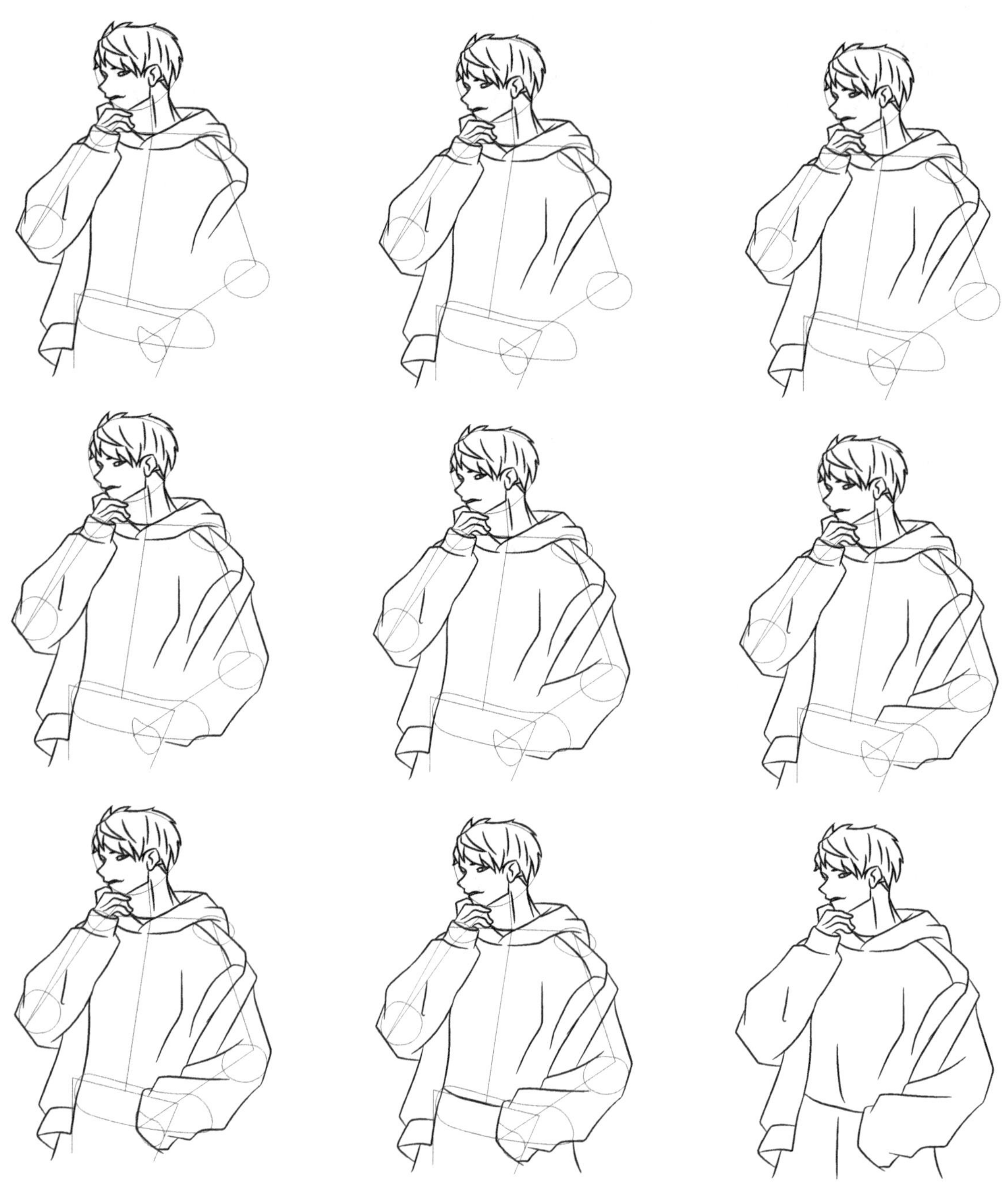

A B C D E F G H
1 2 3 4 5 6 7 8 9 10 11 12

6. Giving your character large eyes and a small nose will make your character look more innocent and childlike.

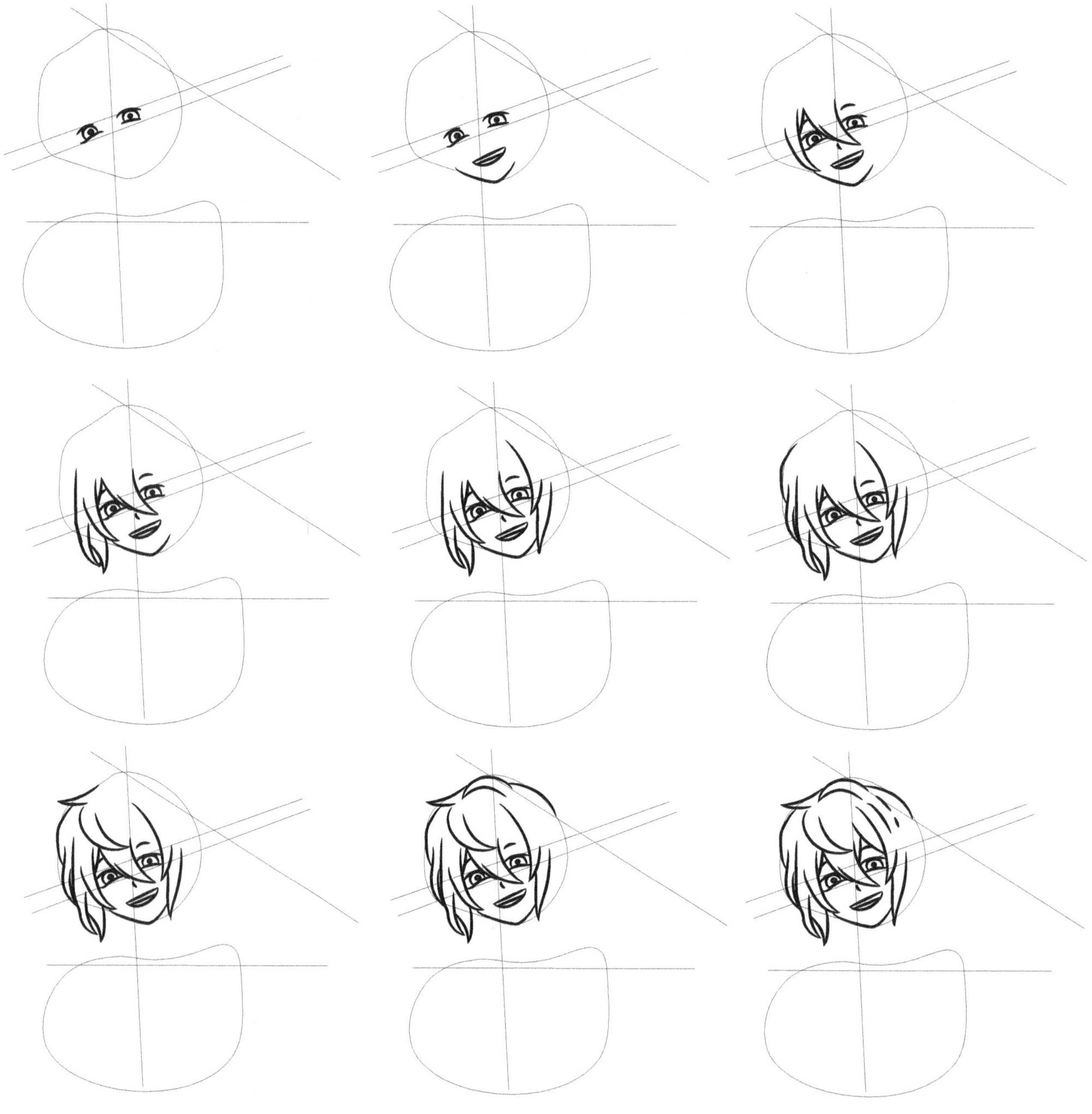

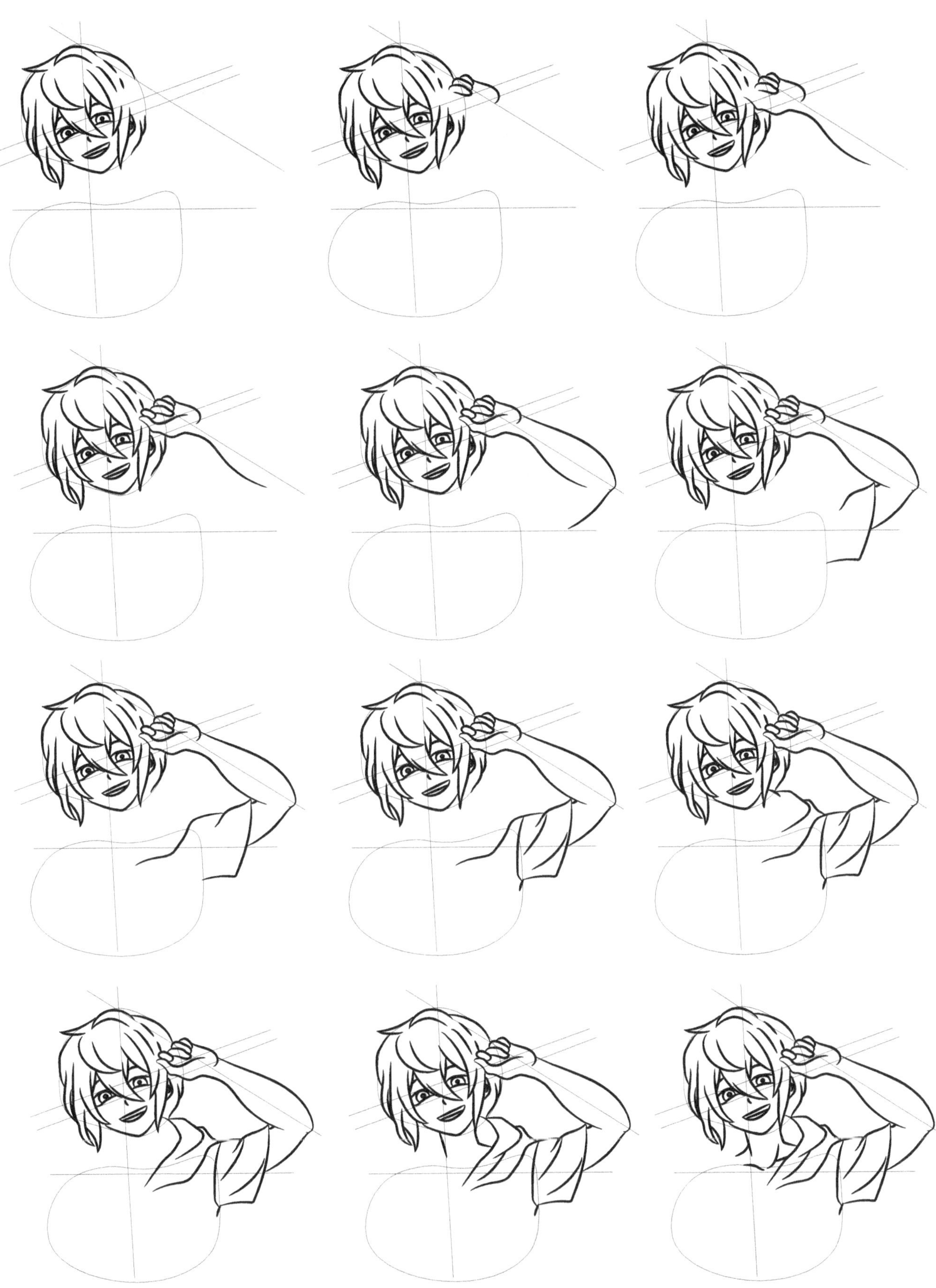

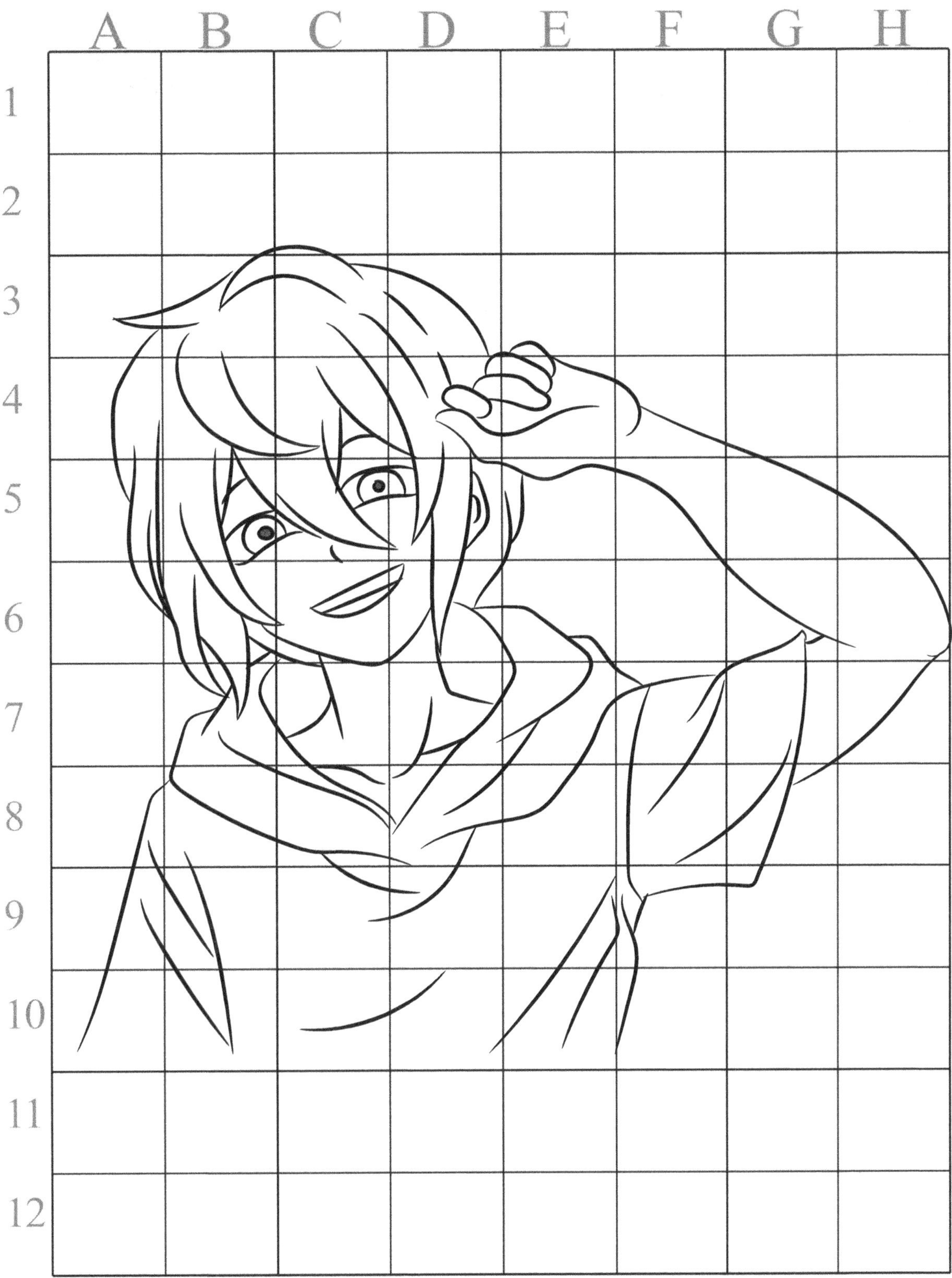

A B C D E F G H
1
2
3
4
5
6
7
8
9
10
11
12

7. You can create 3D type
effects by enlarging some
body parts and making other
body parts smaller.

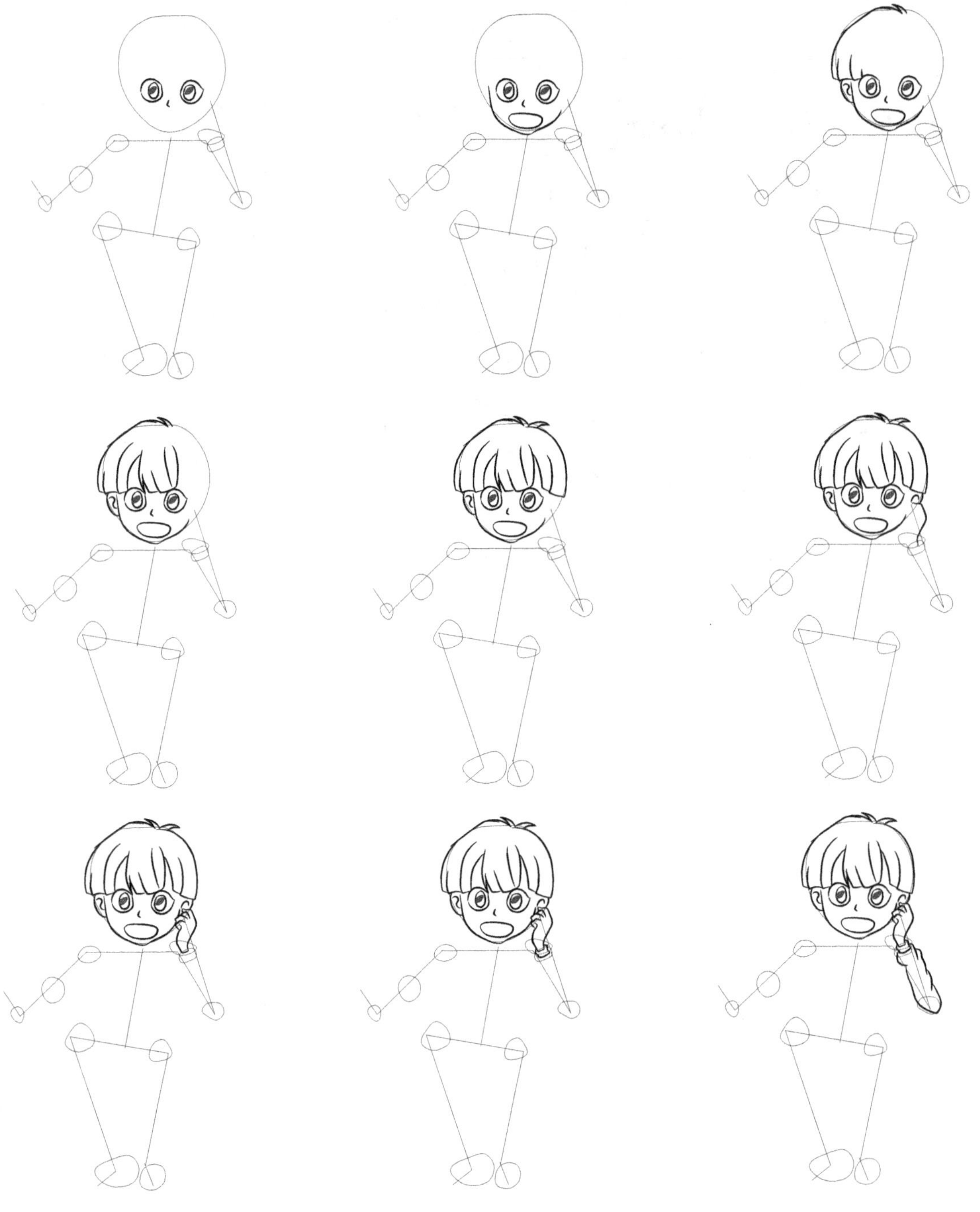

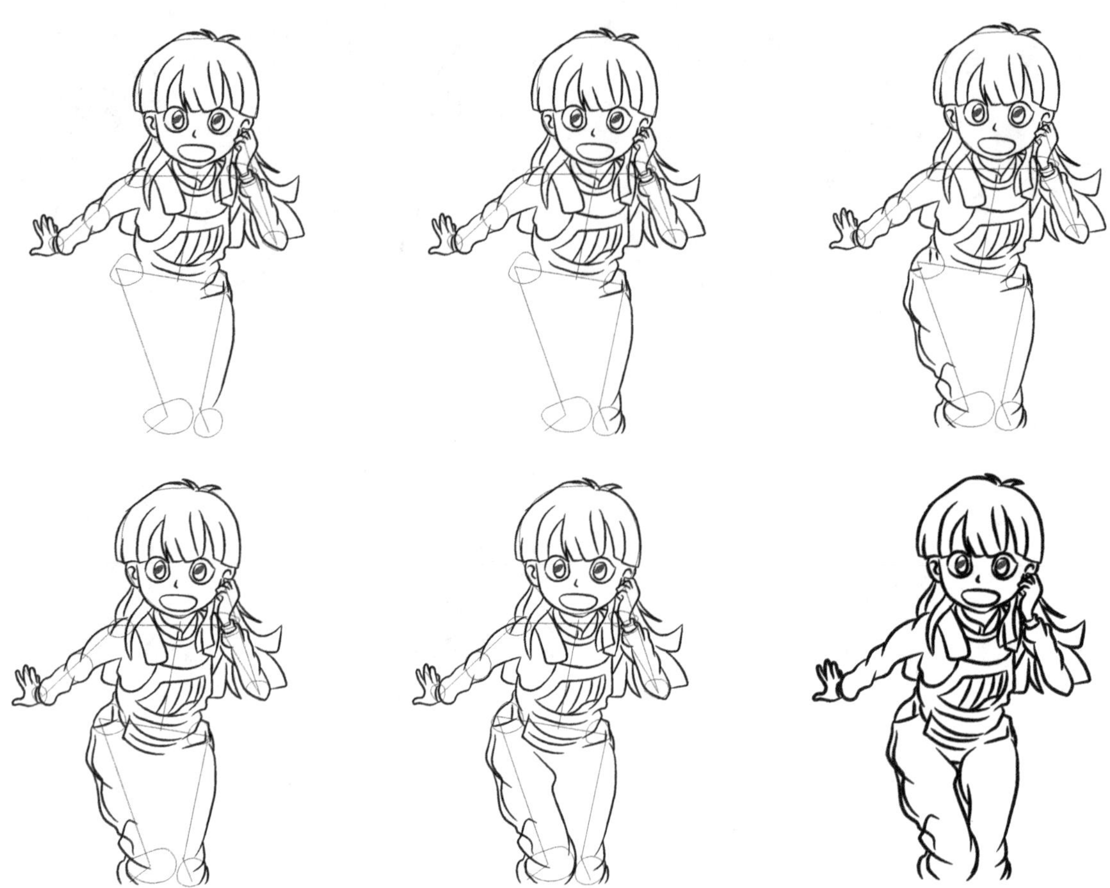

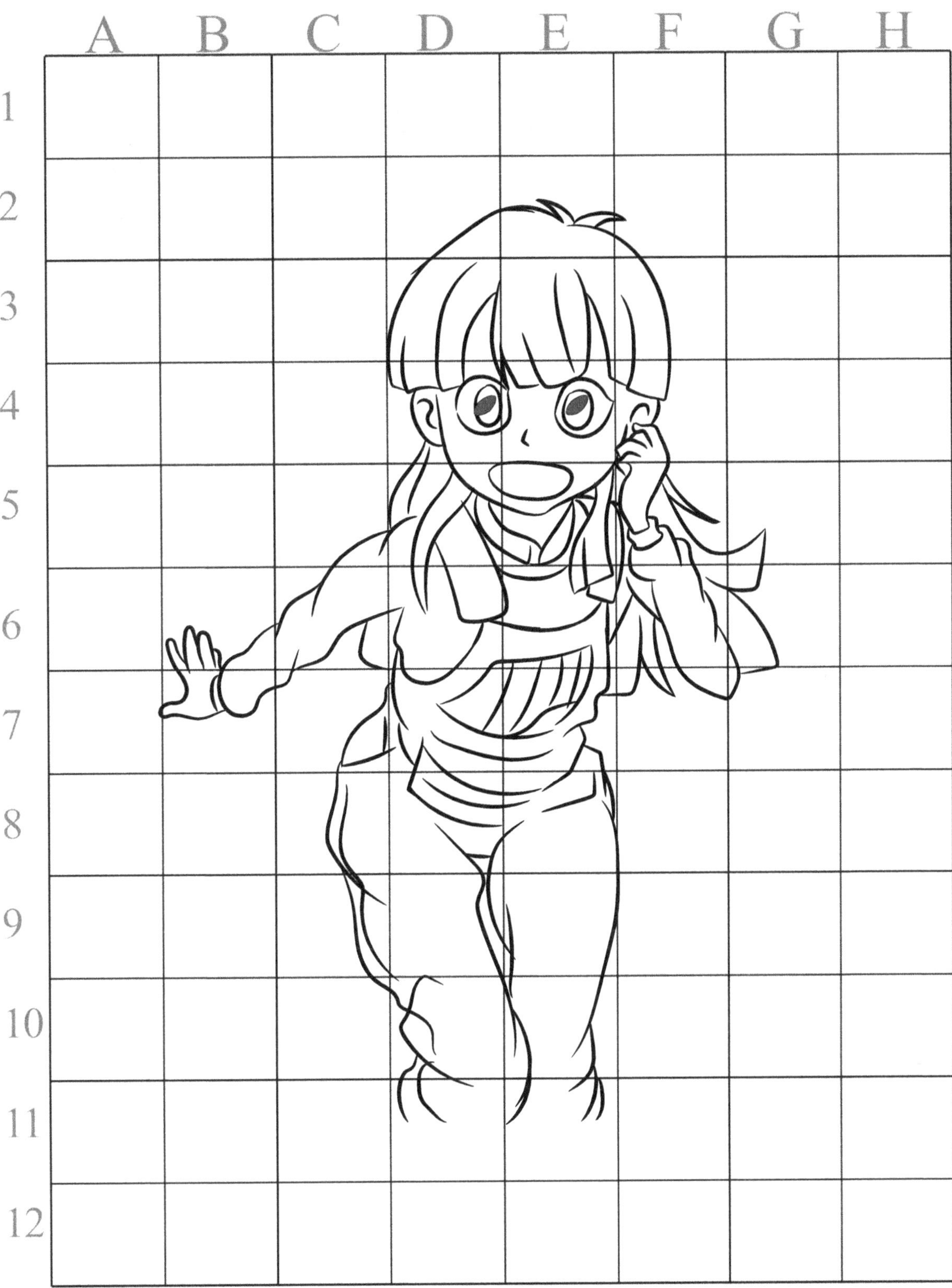

8. Placing eyebrows close to the eyes and making the eyes close together can help you to convey anger.

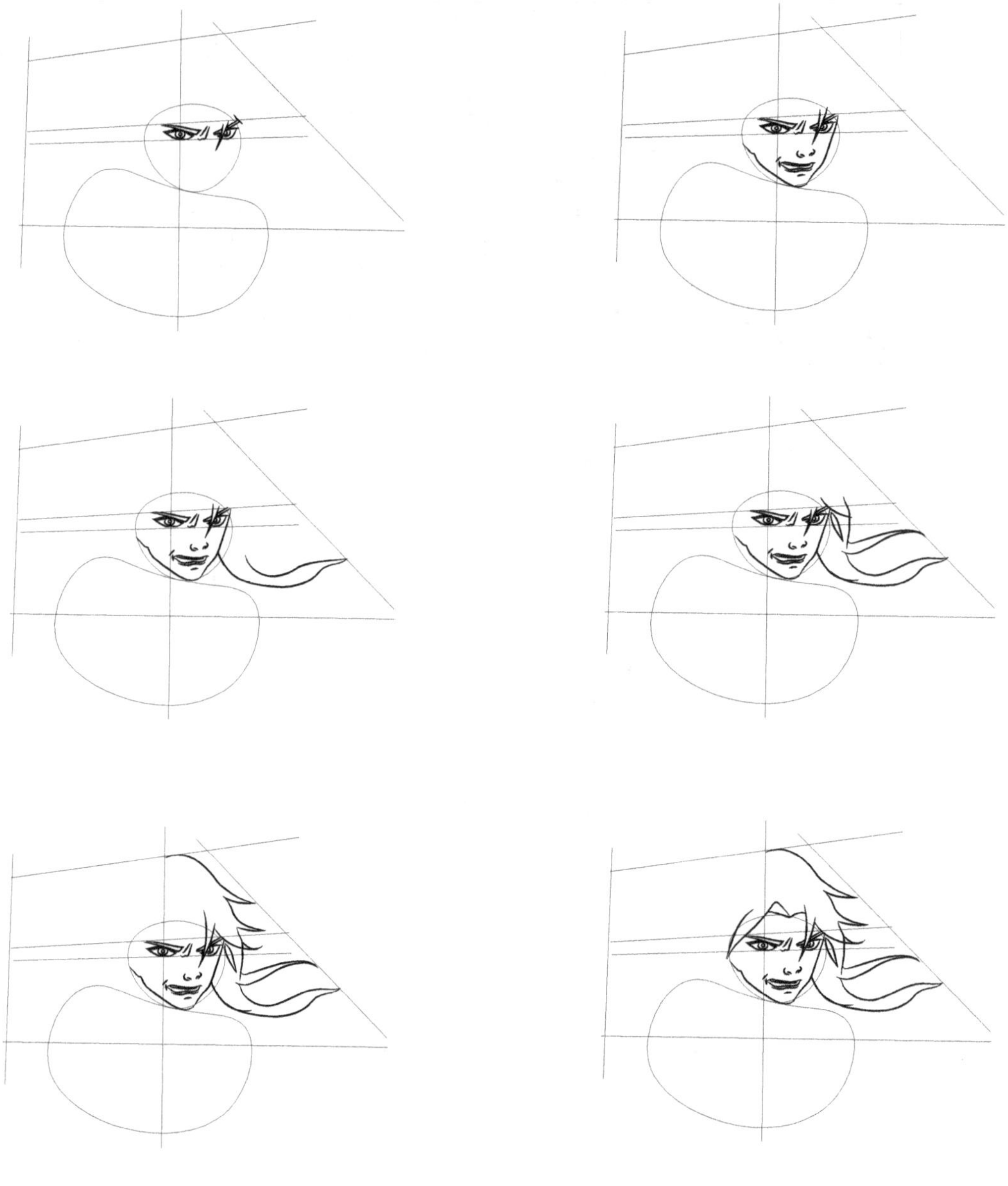

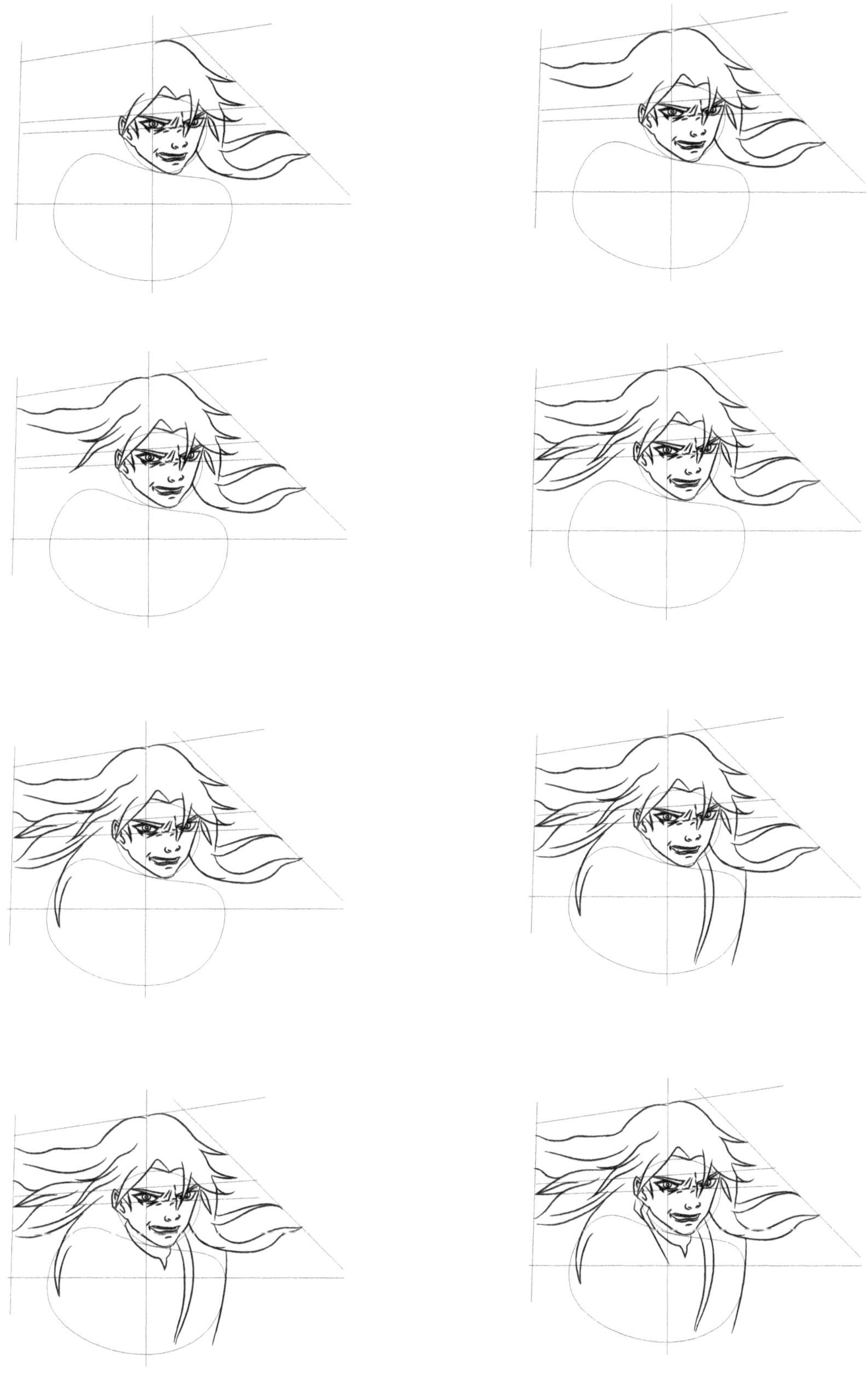

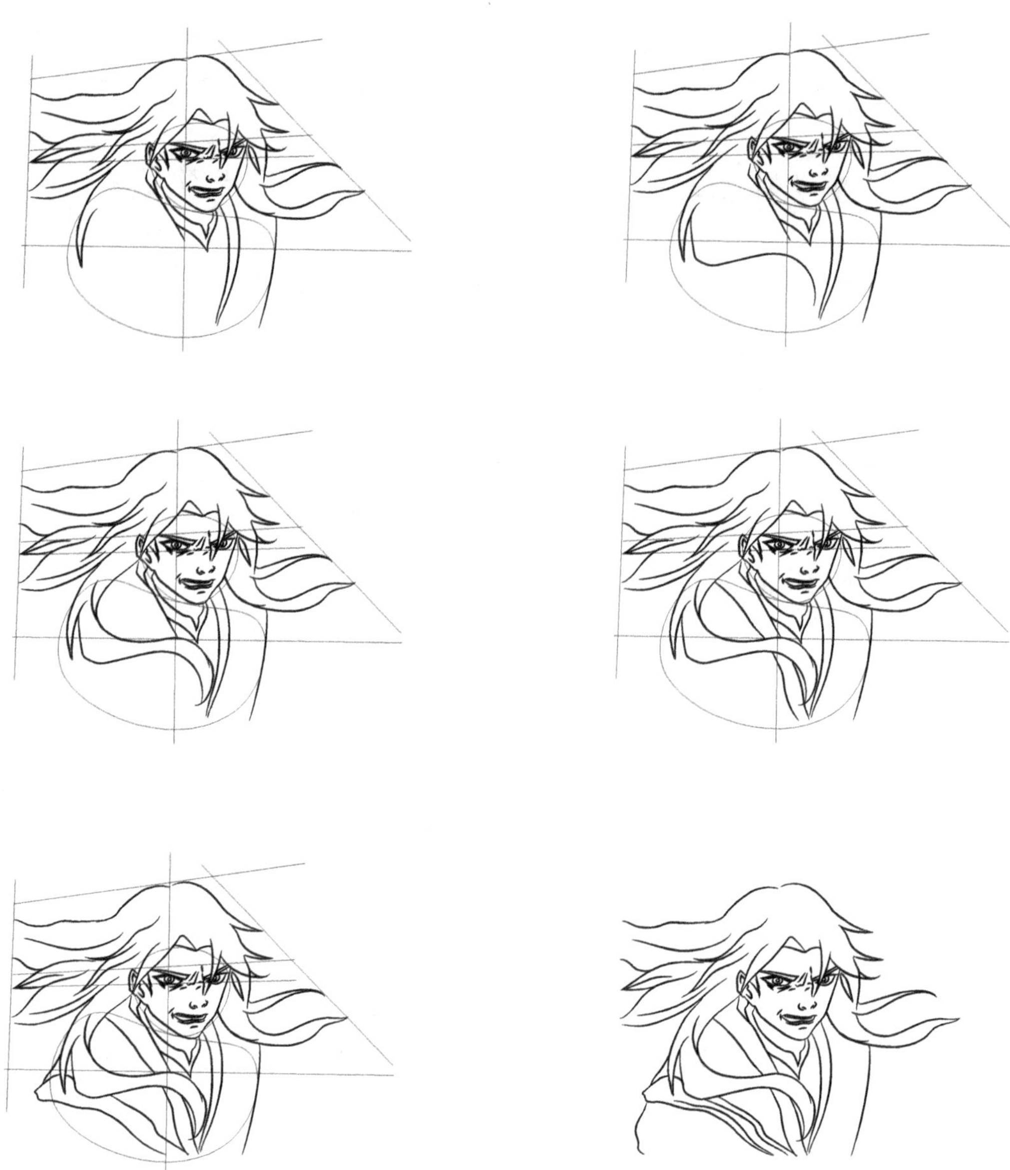

9. To convey sadness have your characters looking down with closed body language. For example, you could draw your characters with their heads down and with their arms crossed.

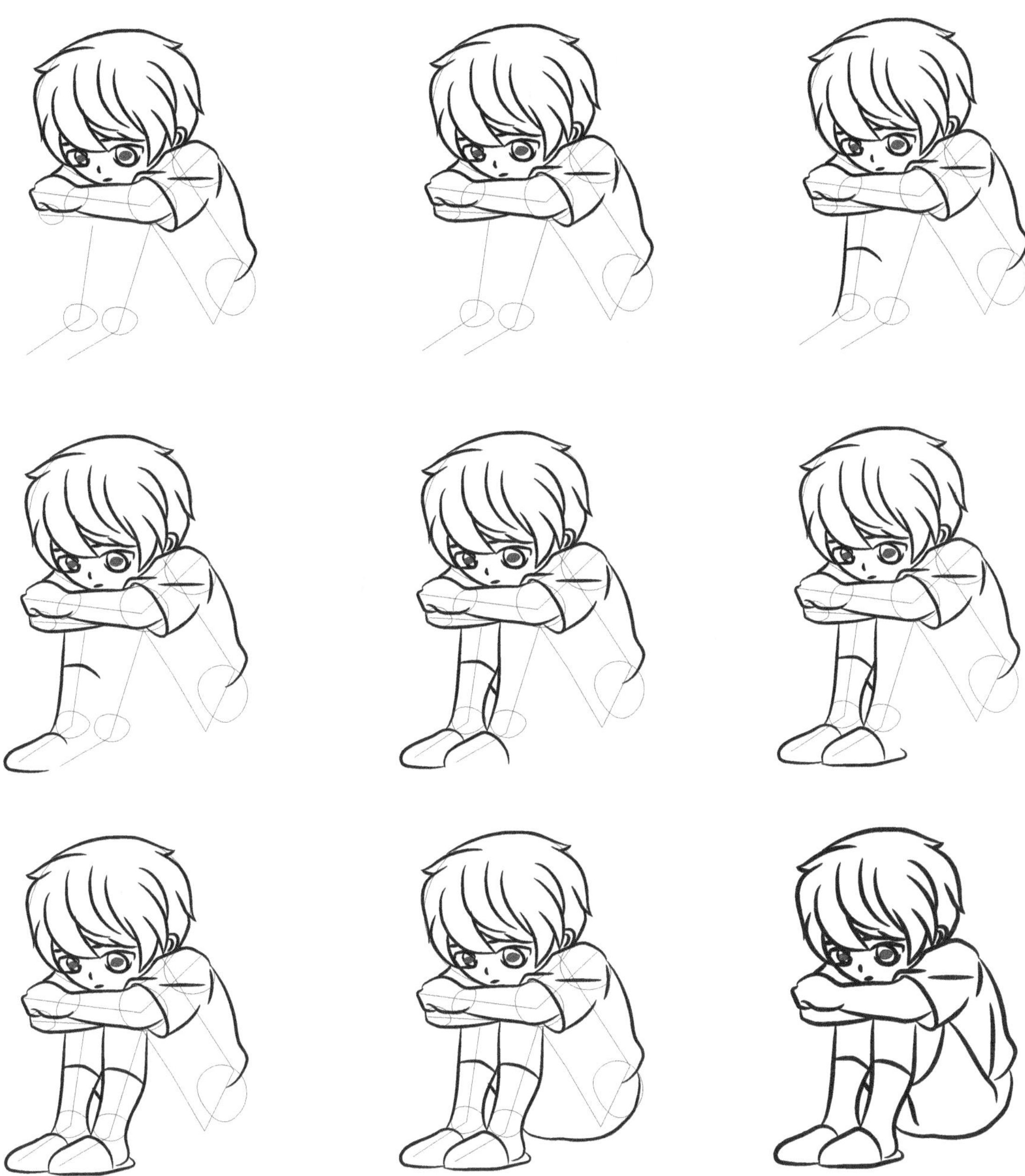

10. If you find that you are rushing, stop what you are doing and take a break. Rushing too much will reduce the quality of your work.

11. If you are struggling for ideas for your work, take a break and do something different. Your mind will keep working in the background for you. Some of our greatest ideas come to us while we sleep.

40

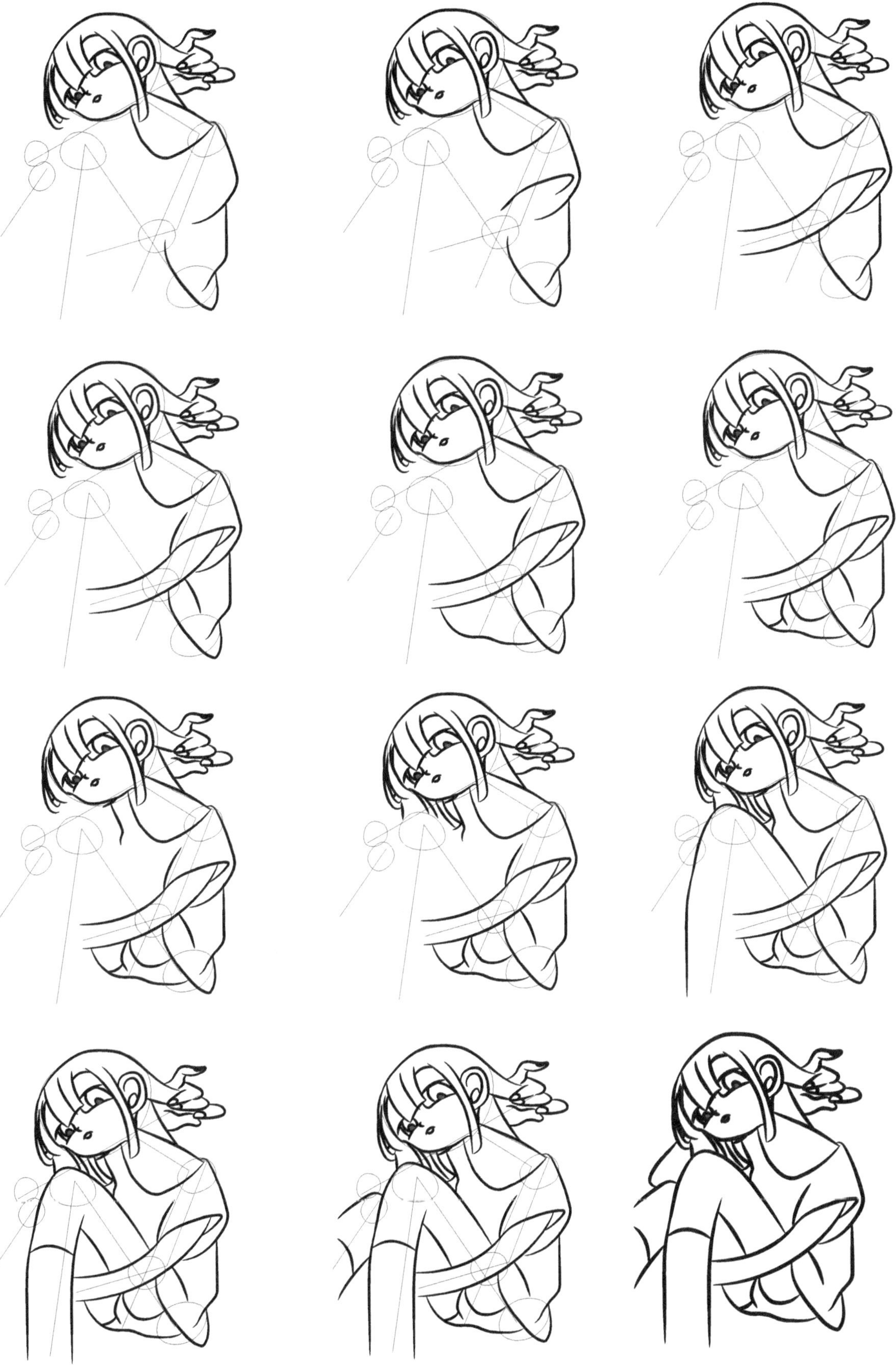

A B C D E F G H
1
2
3
4
5
6
7
8
9
10
11
12

12. You can create the appearance
of characters keeping their
thoughts to themselves by crossing
their arms and having them look
ahead.

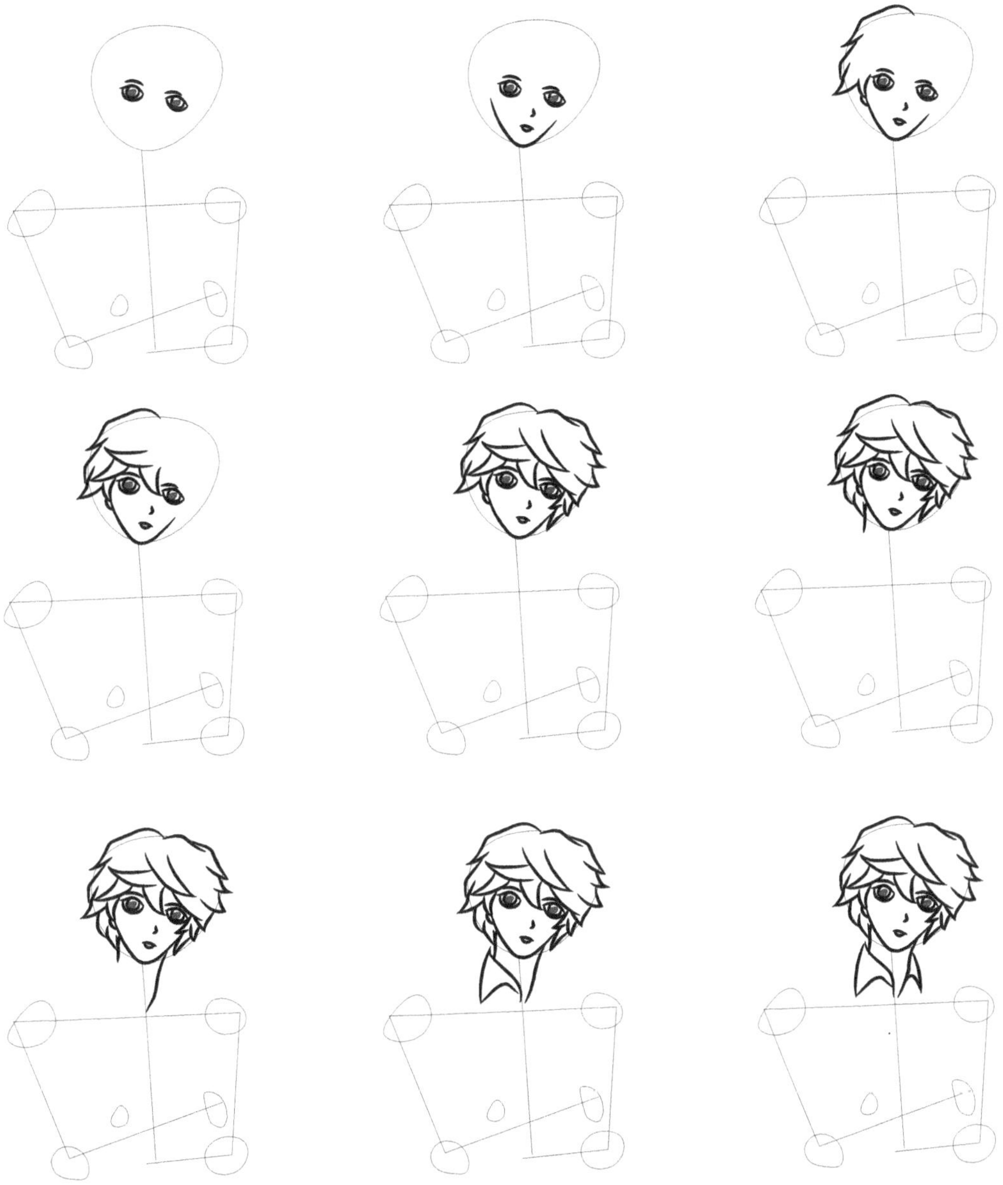

13. You can make your character look surprised or shocked by increasing the distance between the eyes and the eyebrows.

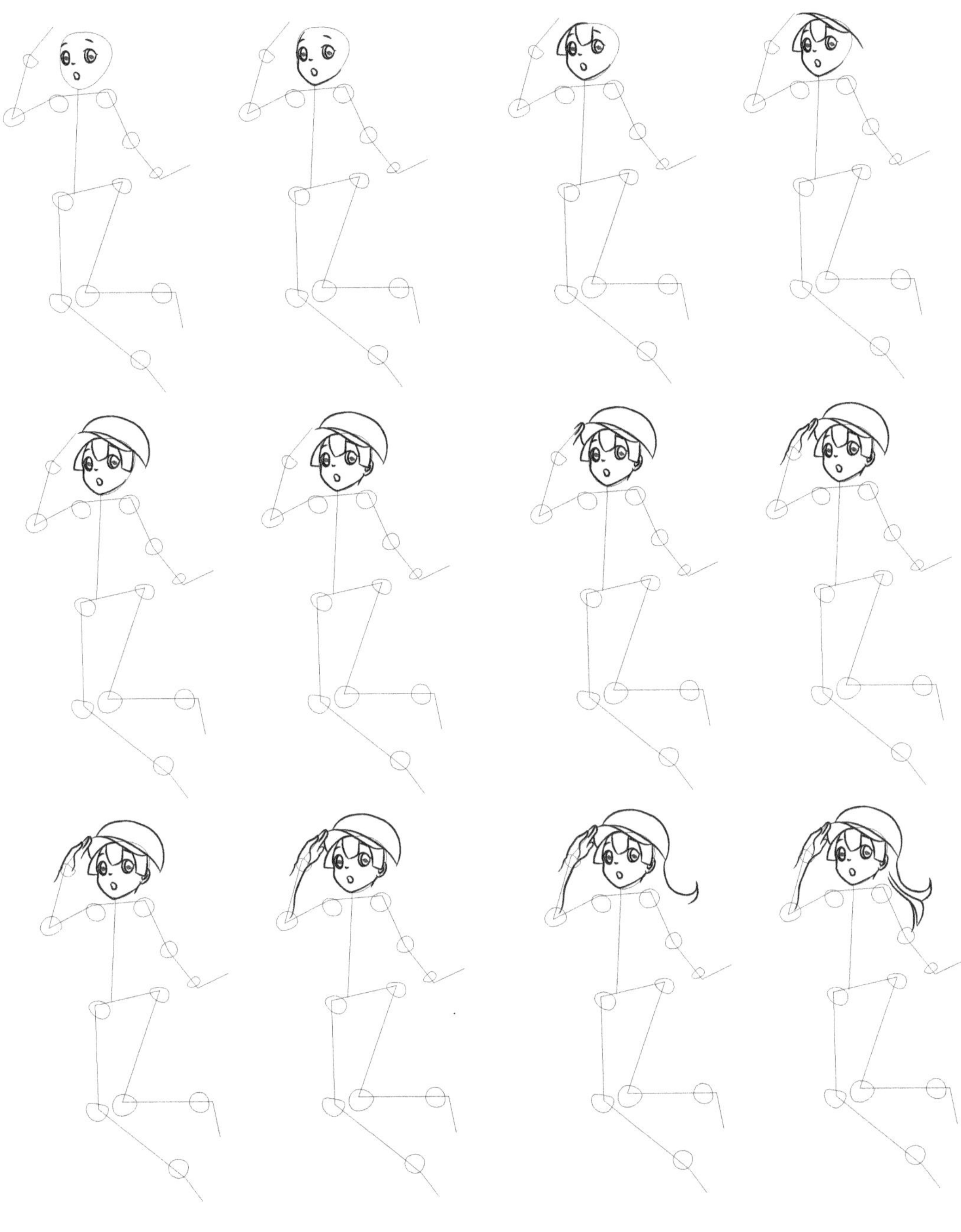

A B C D E F G H

14. You can make your characters look as though they have a point to make about something by raising their index finger in comparison with their other fingers.

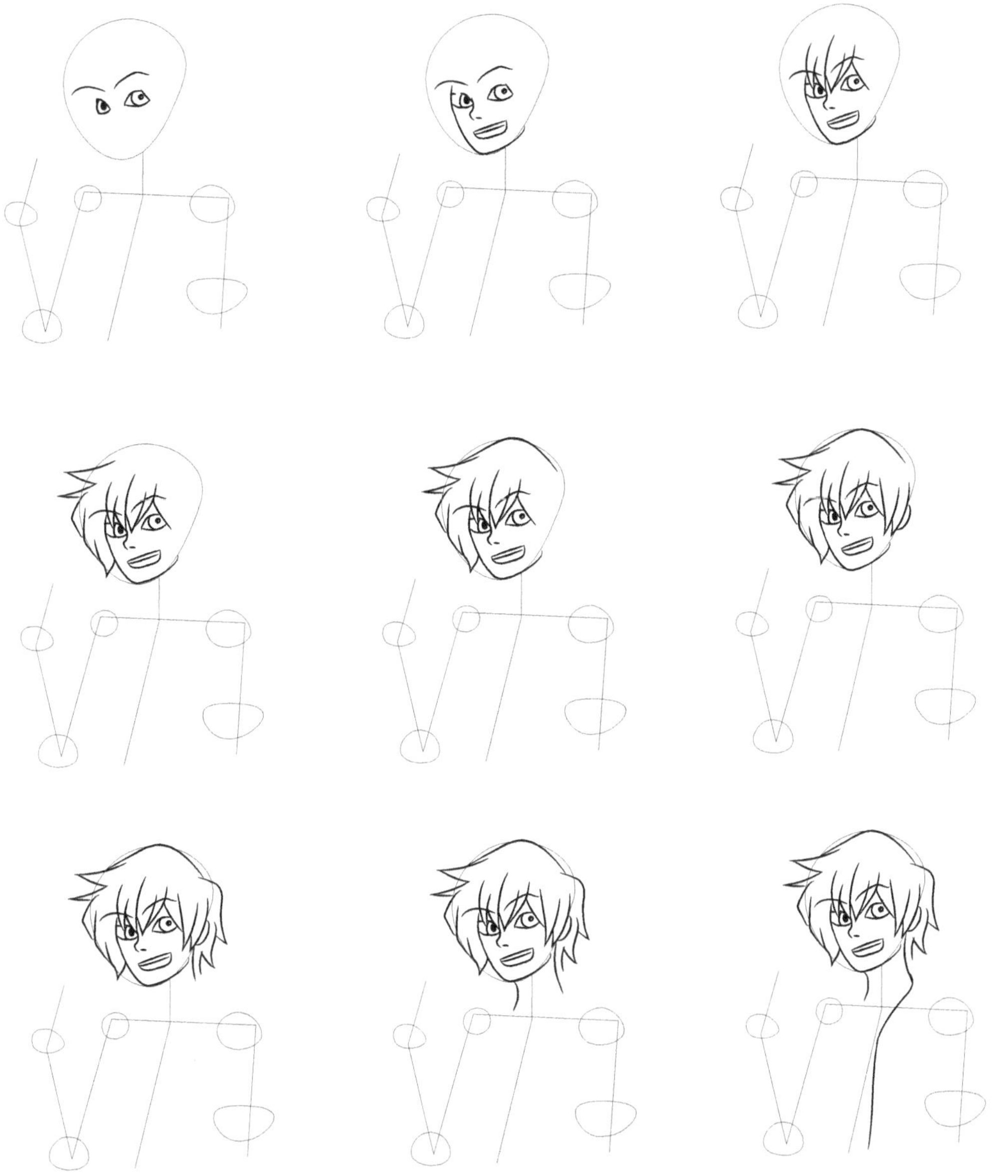

15. When we have slight reservations we may cross our body with one arm while keeping the other arm open.

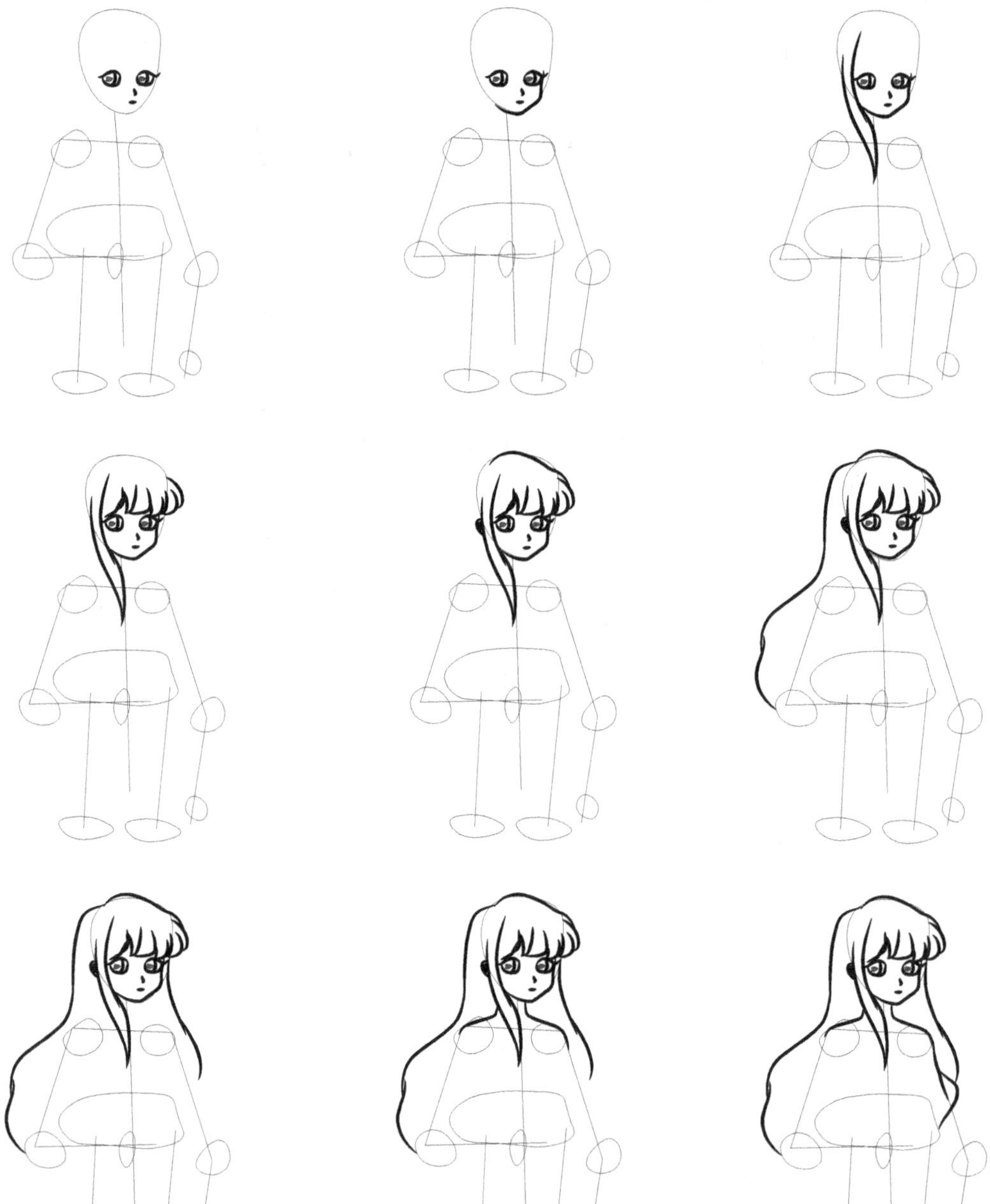

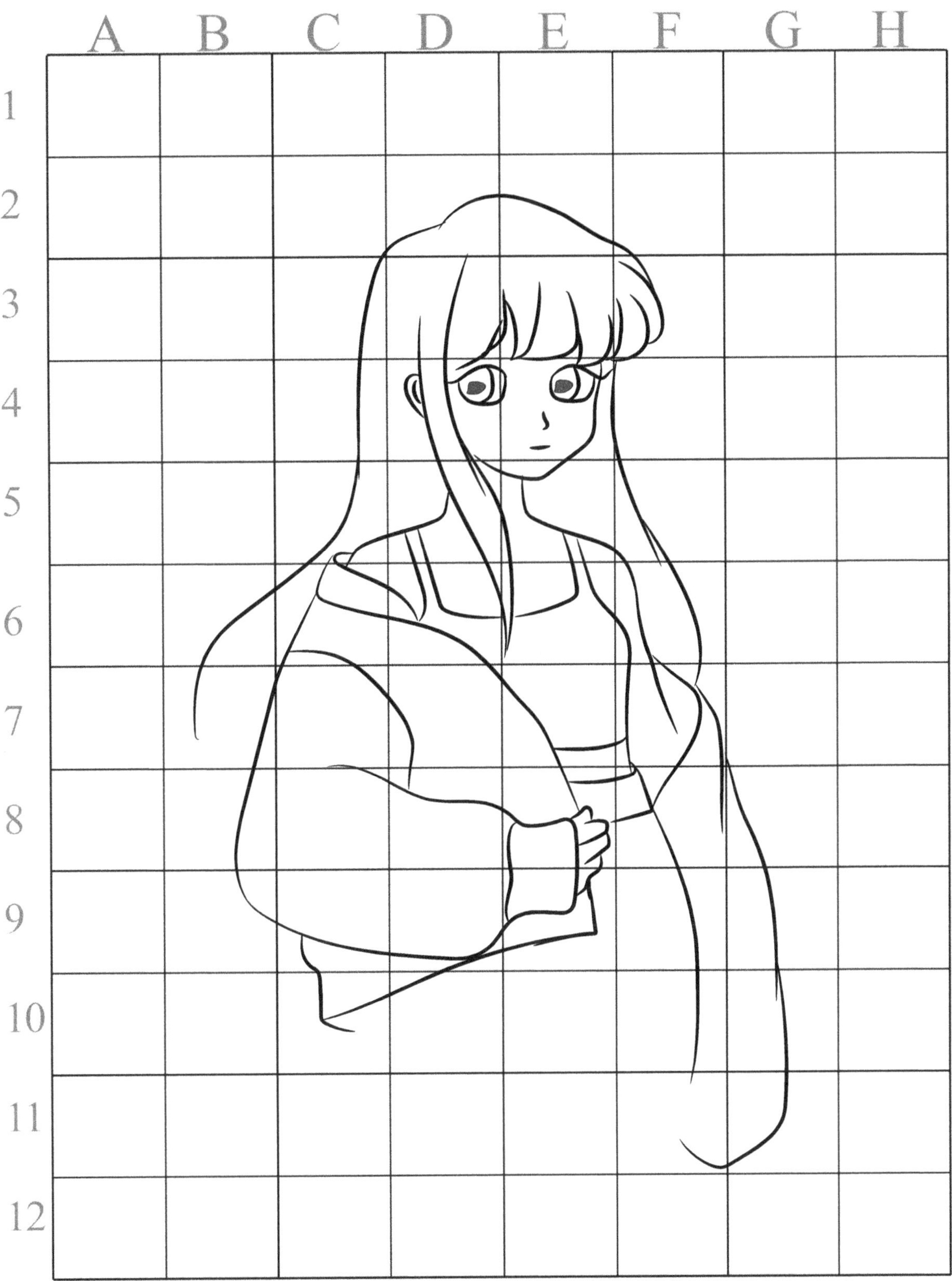

A B C D E F G H
1
2
3
4
5
6
7
8
9
10
11
12

16. It can be very difficult to get things right the first time, but remember the more you draw the better you will get at it.

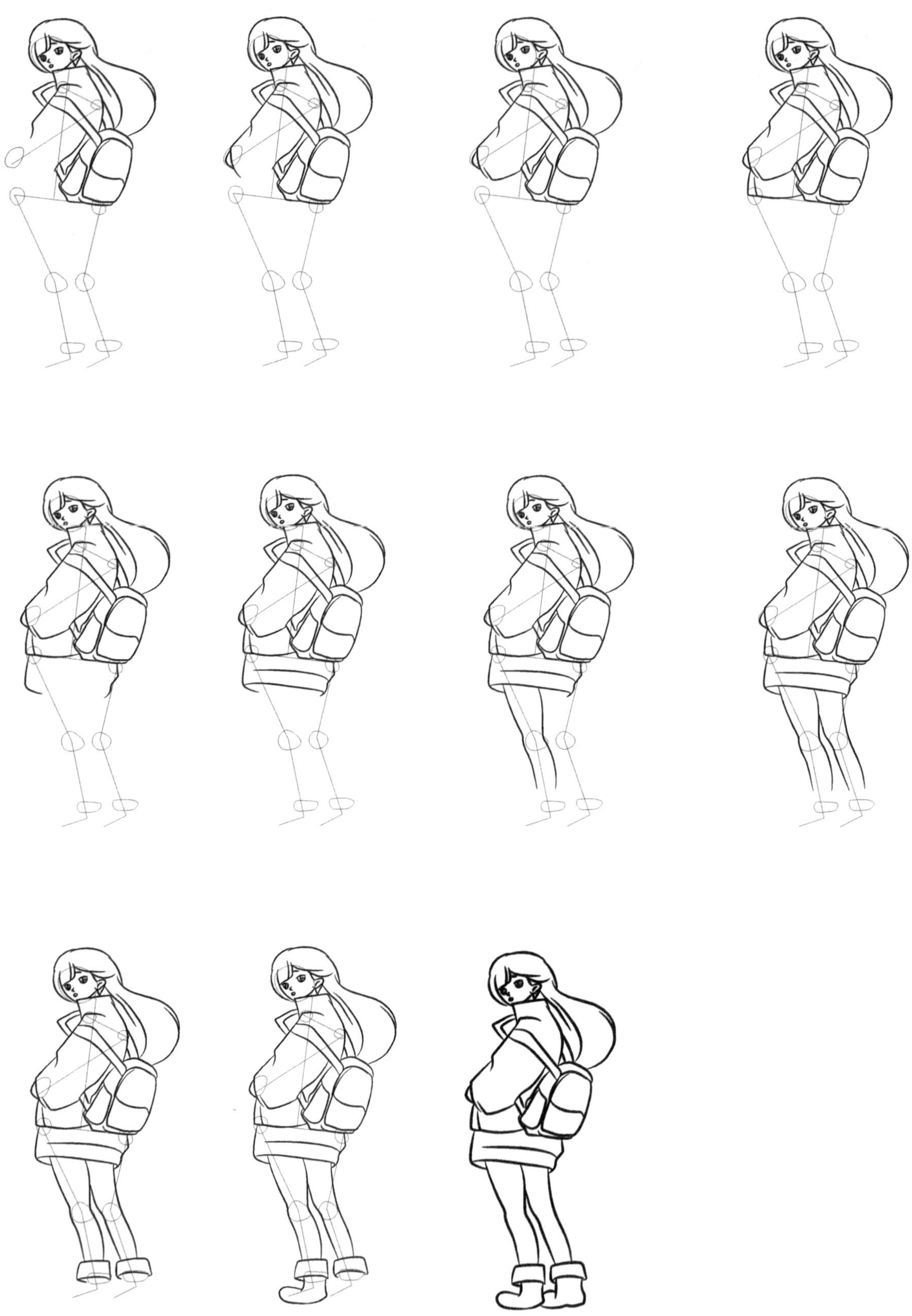

A B C D E F G H
1
2
3
4
5
6
7
8
9
10
11
12

17. Building a basic stick character can often
be a useful way to get yourself started.

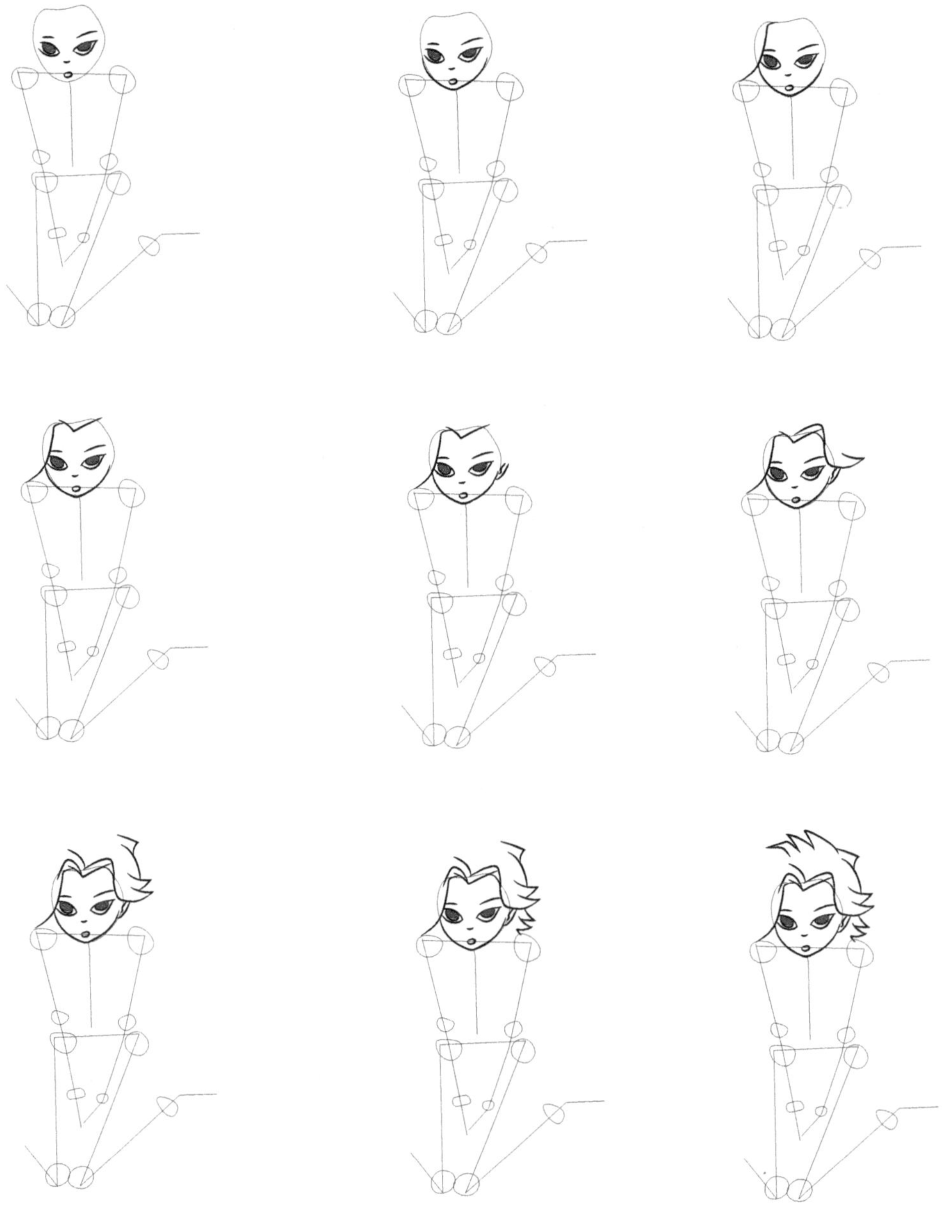

18. Giving your character large eyes and a small nose and mouth will make your character look more innocent and childlike.

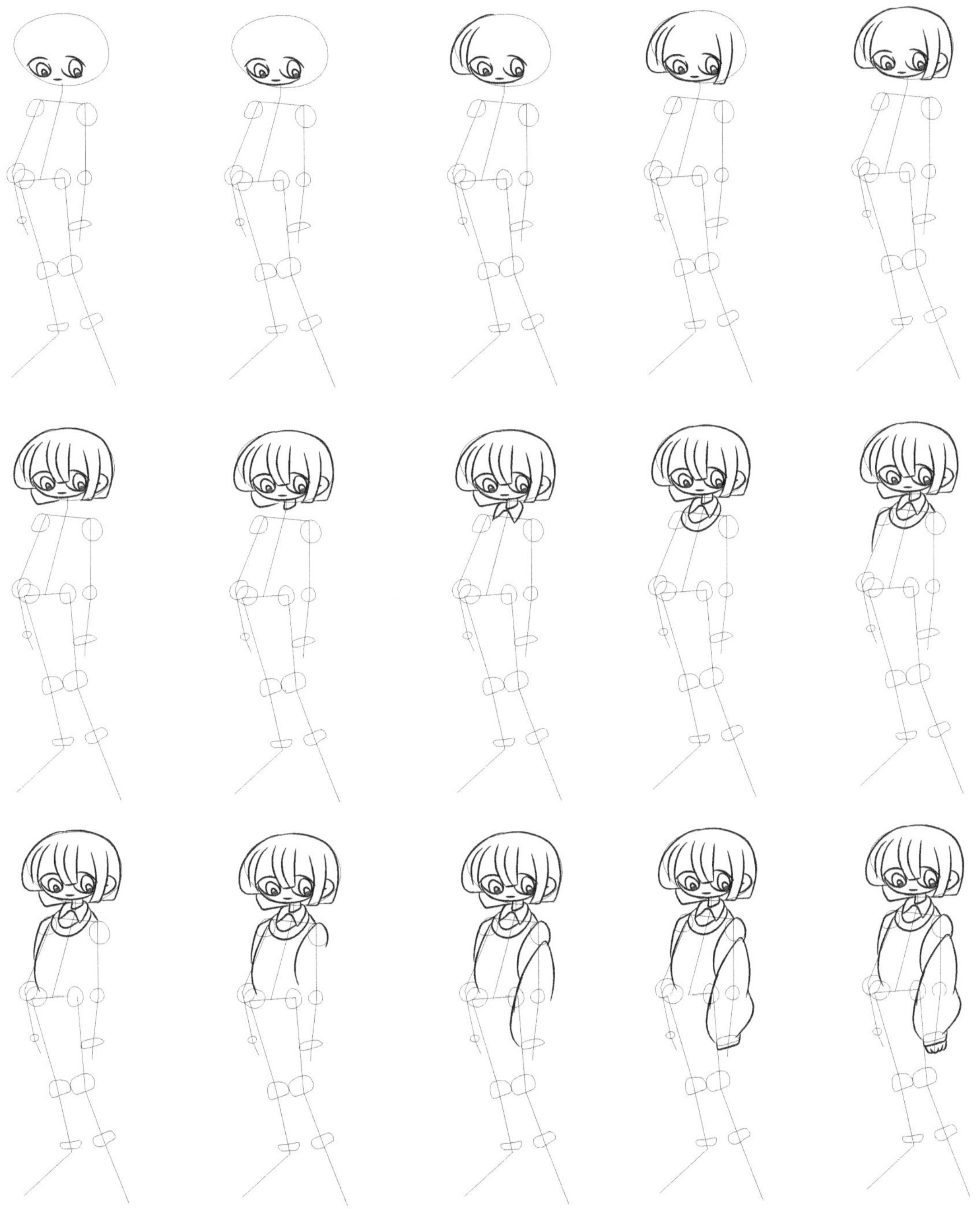

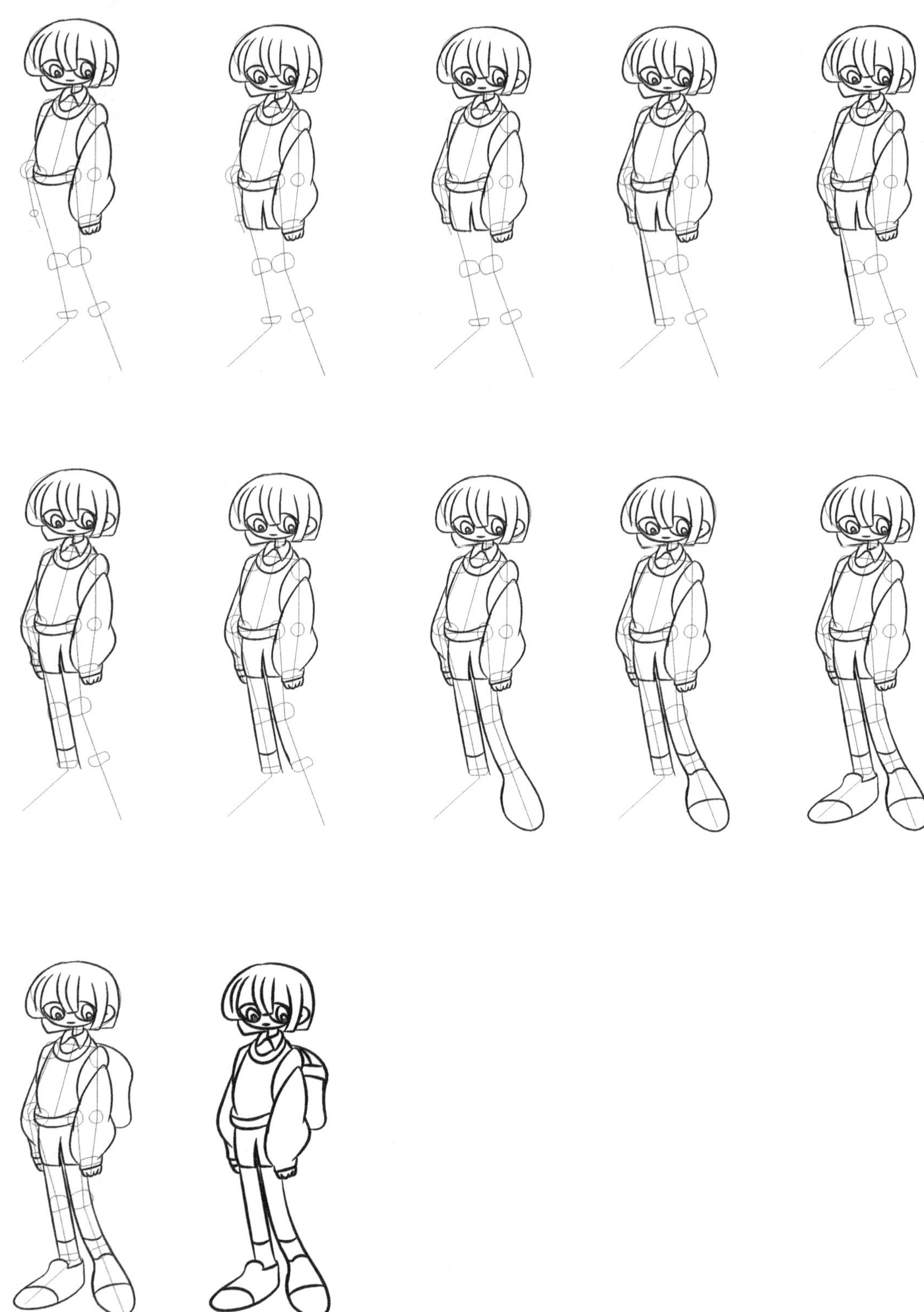

19. If a project looks too difficult to complete
all in one go, complete part of it and come
back to it a little later. It will then feel less
overwhelming.

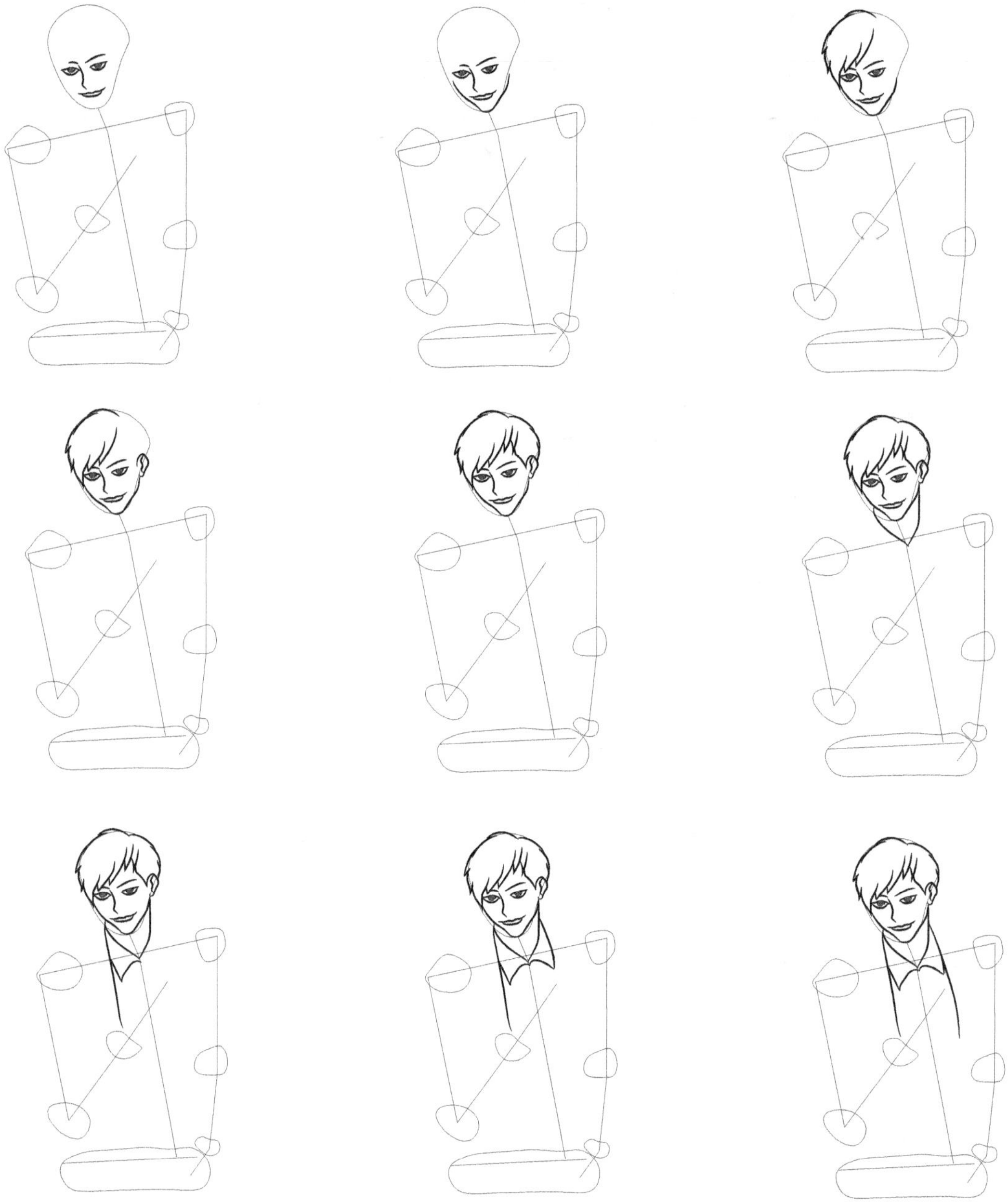

A B C D E F G H
1
2
3
4
5
6
7
8
9
10
11
12

20. If you are struggling for ideas for your work, take a break and do something different. Your mind will keep working in the background for you. Some of our greatest ideas come to us while we sleep.

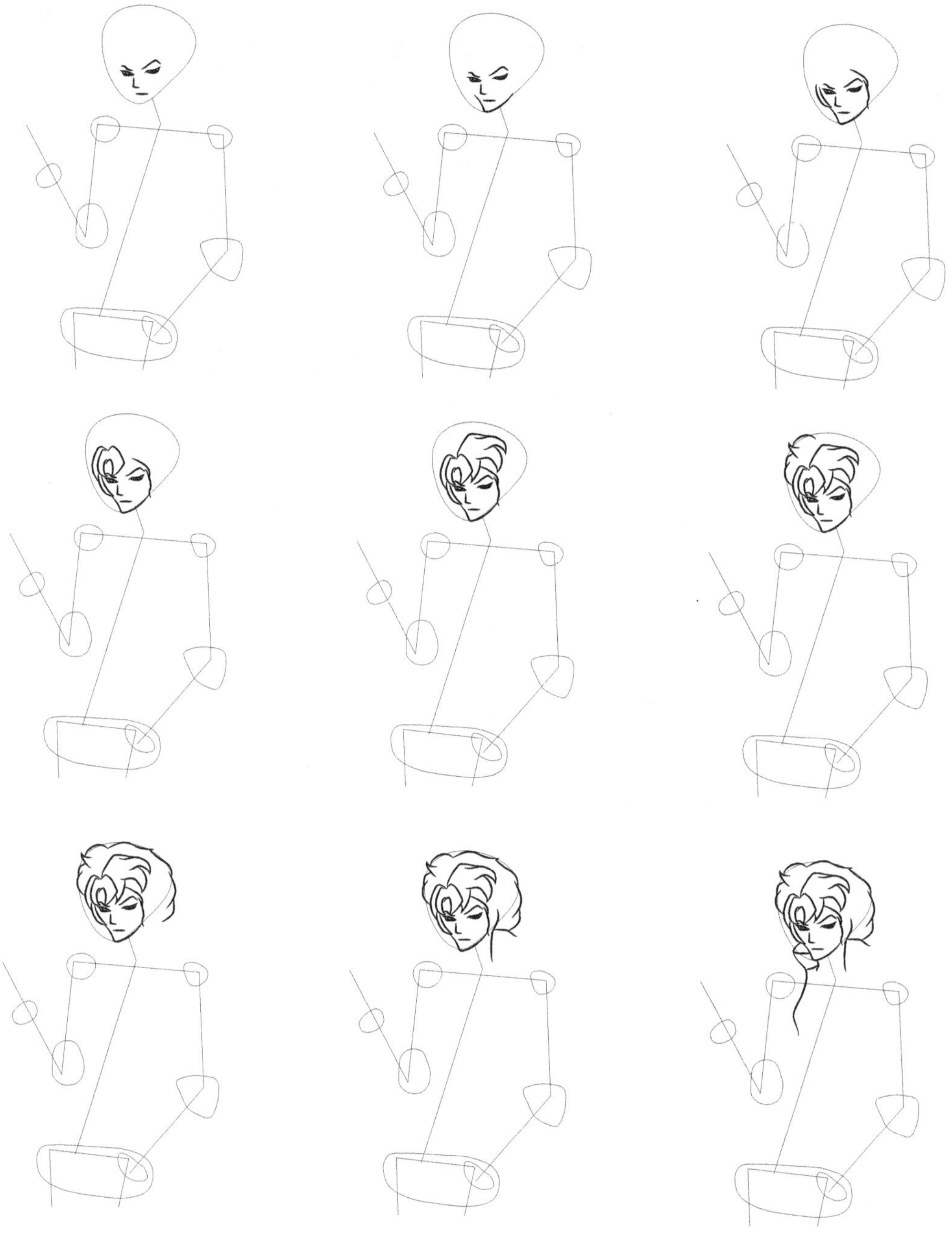

www.ingramcontent.com/pod-product-compliance
Lightning Source LLC
Chambersburg PA
CBHW081227130726
47997CB00009B/2803